F

"I have asked for God's forgiveness and I feel cleaner before God than I have ever felt."
—Sandi Patty

"I'm trying to learn how to pray without ceasing—it's something the Bible tells us to do."
—Carolyn Arends

"We are never alone, regardless of our struggles. Nothing can separate us from the love of God no matter how distant we may feel from Him. So we have nothing to hide, lose, fear, or ever prove. God's love saved us from sin, so it can—and will—rescue us from our daily trials as well."
—Geoff Moore

"For me, Scripture is the light to the path."
—Eddie Carswell

"The goal is that you should be like Jesus—and the Scriptures can help you with that. I don't read the Bible because I'm a great saint. I read the Bible because I'll find God there. It's about a daily walk with this person Jesus."
—Rich Mullins

Other contributors include:

Bruce Carroll • Bryan Duncan • Kathy Troccoli • Larnelle Harris • Lisa Bragg • Margaret Becker • Neal Coomer • Randy Phillips • Rebecca St. James • Tony Vincent

ALSO BY LES SUSSMAN

Miracles Can Happen
Yes, Lord, I'm Coming Home

Les Sussman

Praise Him!

Christian Music Stars Share Their
Favorite Verses from the Scriptures

B

BERKLEY BOOKS, NEW YORK

Lyrics on p. 96 from "You First Loved Me" by Lisa Daggs
reprinted by permission of the author.

PRAISE HIM! CHRISTIAN MUSIC STARS SHARE
THEIR FAVORITE VERSES FROM THE SCRIPTURES

A Berkley Book / published by arrangement with
St. Martin's Press, Inc.

PRINTING HISTORY
St. Martin's edition / May 1998
Berkley trade paperback edition / June 1999

All rights reserved.
Copyright © 1998 by Les Sussman.
This book may not be reproduced in whole or in part,
by mimeograph or any other means, without permission.
For information address:
St. Martin's Press, Inc., 175 Fifth Avenue,
New York, New York 10010.

The Penguin Putnam Inc. World Wide Web site address is
http://www.penguinputnam.com

ISBN: 0-425-16867-0

BERKLEY®
Berkley Books are published by
The Berkley Publishing Group, a division of Penguin Putnam Inc.,
375 Hudson Street, New York, New York 10014.
BERKLEY and the "B" design are trademarks
belonging to Penguin Putnam Inc.

PRINTED IN THE UNITED STATES OF AMERICA

10 9 8 7 6 5 4 3 2 1

To all who seek

the Real behind the seeming

Contents

Author's Note   ix

Acknowledgments   xiii

Sandi Patty   1

Bruce Carroll   11

Bryan Duncan   23

Carolyn Arends   35

Geoff Moore   45

John Schlitt   55

Kathy Troccoli   63

Larnelle Harris   73

Lisa Bragg   83

Lisa Daggs   93

Margaret Becker   105

Neal Coomer   115

Eddie Carswell   125

Randy Phillips   135

Rebecca St. James   145

Rich Mullins   155

Tony Vincent   165

Author's Note

THIS BOOK IS THE CROWN OF A God-centered trilogy. My first book in this spiritual series examined the phenomenon of modern-day miracles, while the second dealt with the theme of renewed faith. *Praise Him!* the third and final one, focuses on the power of scripture to change our lives.

As an author who began his writing career as a newspaperman, I'm quite grateful that God has allowed me the opportunity to write on subjects of much more importance than murder, rape, and the latest political scandal.

We're just around the corner from a new millennium, and everywhere we look there seems to be fresh evidence that a spiritual renaissance is under way—from the plethora of television shows and movies about angels to the tremendous increase in belief in God, according to the latest Gallop polls.

And I'm glad that through my books I can be contributing in some small measure to this resurgence in spiritual consciousness.

The Christian artists whose favorite scriptures appear in this book have long been in the vanguard of this spiritual movement, sometimes at great professional and personal cost. They are all very talented, and many easily could have found work earning big dollars with secular labels.

Instead, they chose commitment over commercialism—singing beautifully inspiring songs that offer homage to God's love and grace. It may be awhile before their work is ever seen on MTV, but I know that they all have the satisfaction of their music being listened to by a much higher authority.

Although over the years I've had the opportunity to interview many celebrities, I must add that as a set, Christian music stars are among the most earnest, soul-searching group of entertainers that I have ever had the privilege of knowing. These are committed men and women who are just as deeply connected to the Lord offstage as on.

Each artist who appears in this book was asked to choose his or her favorite scripture and to share with readers why it was selected. What emerges is an uplifting collection of stories of the role scripture has played in helping them to overcome obstacles in their lives.

My fervent hope is that by reading these stories, you, too,

will find the inspiration, encouragement, and hope you are seeking. Above all, I wish you deep faith and all of God's blessings.

Les Sussman
New York City
July 11, 1997

Acknowledgments

JUST AS IT TAKES MANY VOICES to strengthen the power of prayer, this book was enhanced by the participation of many kind people who contributed their time and energy—from the artists to their publicists and managers. My heartfelt gratitude to each and every one of them.

While space prohibits me from listing everyone I would like to thank, special gratitude is due the following:

Ray Ware, Mark Schmidt; David Schraeder; Gina Adams and Myra Sumner of The Adams Group; Paula Haggard; Atkins, Muse & Associates; Rendy Lovelady Management; Creative Trust; Marita Meinerts; and Mike Keil (John Schlitt's manager), who was responsible for the launch of this book.

Major debts of gratitude also to my editor, Jim Fitzgerald,

one of the few New Yorkers who is knowledgeable about Christian music; Claire Gerus, my good friend, agent, and spiritual confidante; and the always helpful people at the Gospel Music Association and *CCM Magazine*.

And last but not least, my special friends—Alan and Andrea, Sally, Patricia, Judith, and Karyn—who always seem to be available when I need them.

Sandi Patty

. . . If ye continue in my word, then *are ye my disciples indeed; and ye shall know the truth, and the truth shall make you free.*

JOHN 8:31-32

SANDI PATTY'S WORLD WAS SHATtered in 1995 when her millions of adoring fans learned the shocking news that the internationally acclaimed Christian music superstar had been involved in an extramarital affair.

Particularly disturbing to her fans was that this incredibly talented singer and songwriter had, over the years, carefully cultivated a pro-family image.

When Sandi, the winner of an incredible thirty-four Dove and five Grammy awards, finally broke her silence on the subject, more shock waves reverberated through the world of Christian music.

The blond, blue-eyed Oklahoma native revealed that she had been sexually abused as a child and cited such abuse as a contributing factor toward the failure of her marriage and her subsequent affair.

Today Sandi recalls those days as one of the most trying times in her life. Not only was the possessor of three platinum and five gold albums spurned by her fans, but many Christian music radio programmers stopped playing her music. In addition, some retailers refused to carry her albums.

The Word Records star praises the verse from John and its message of speaking the truth for aiding her return to wholeness. It's a verse, she offers, that encouraged her to admit her mistakes publicly and to hold herself accountable to her family, church, and fans.

"I will always carry scars, because I know I let lots of people down," Sandi declares. "But when your world feels shattered, you have to begin rebuilding. You can stay where you are broken or you can choose to move on and build something better by God's grace.

"And one way to do so is by being honest. I have asked for God's forgiveness and I feel clearer before God than I ever have felt. As the scripture states, the truth always sets you free."

HAVING LEARNED SOME PAINFUL LESSONS IN RE-cent years, Sandi Patty attests that she is now prepared to move on with her career—one that has produced more than 11 million in record sales since she began performing fifteen years ago.

Although the Christian music superstar who once per-formed at the White House for the president and first lady acknowledges that she continues to heal, it has not kept her from completing a new Christmas album, while preparing a concert schedule that includes everything from performing at pop concerts to appearances with major national and inter-national symphony orchestras.

Sandi, who resides in Anderson, Indiana, with her fitness-instructor husband, Don Peslis, and eight children, is also keeping busy teaching music at Anderson University.

Behind this flurry of activity is a desire to get on with her life and not abandon her remarkable, God-given talent that has made Sandi one of the nation's best-loved performers. Sandi also hopes that by rebuilding her own life, she will serve as a symbol of encouragement to others who have suffered hard times.

"God has walked me through some incredibly difficult times, and now I'm on the other side of it," she declares earnestly. "I want to share God's love and joy with anyone who is struggling with the realities of life."

Sandi believes she is on the right track, and describes an experience that she construes as a sign of approval from the Lord. That incident took place when the entertainer and her husband arrived at a local hospital to bring home Samuel, a baby boy they had recently adopted.

"You know, Samuel means 'God has heard,'" Sandi explains. "And when we saw him and picked him up from the hospital, the nurses had written his name in a little heart with rainbows around it.

"The first time God gave a rainbow was as a promise that there would never be a storm like that again. So here, after a kind of storm in my life, for us to be entrusted with a child—the promise of a new life, a new beginning—and to see that rainbow, for us today as much as it was for Noah back then it was a sign that God was still with us."

Although Sandi may have stumbled briefly in her walk, the Christian music luminary comes from a family with a deep commitment to God. She was born in Oklahoma City, Oklahoma, the daughter of an Assembly of God minister, and religion was always very much part of her household.

Sandi relates that at age three, she and her family relocated to Phoenix, Arizona. Another move to Sacramento, California, followed. After high school graduation there was yet another move—this time to her current home of Anderson, Indiana, where Sandi attended her church college.

Besides religion, the Christian artist recalls that music also played a big role in her family life. Sandi's father served in various congregations as minister of music, and her mother, when not at home raising the kids, often could be found in church accompanying her husband on the organ.

"Growing up there was not a lot of strong rebellion against my religious upbringing," she submits. "Christianity was a big part of my life, and church was a big part of my life. My heart's desire was always to be a disciple of Christ. I guess I was basically a compliant kid."

Although she always loved to sing, Sandi recollects that being a performer was not her first choice of a career. "I always wanted to be a schoolteacher and teach music," she reveals, "but toward the end of my college years I started to get invited to sing here and sing there and doors really began opening. So I felt that was the direction that God wanted me to go."

In 1978 Sandi married her first husband, John, when they were both students in college. Twelve years later, however, there were major cracks in their marriage.

"I felt rejected time after time by my husband," she asserts. "I was extremely vulnerable—more vulnerable than I ever realized. I needed someone to care, someone to hear me, and someone to listen to me."

Now Sandi tends to place less blame on her husband for the breakup of their marriage and is willing to accept more of the responsibility for its deterioration.

She also speaks openly about the psychological wounds she suffered as a young girl, when she was sexually molested by a female church member.

"I think as I continued to grow and continued to grow closer to the Lord, I realized that there were pretty rough wounds in my life and my childhood from sexual abuse—it was from a woman who was a schoolteacher and sang in my dad's choir.

"Whenever you have those kinds of wounds—especially

when they're unconscious—there's no way to bring whole-ness to a marriage. I think that by the time I realized that, there was just a lot of damage that I brought to the marriage.

"And one of the things that happens when there is sexual abuse, there are literally no boundaries. There are no personal boundaries, friendship boundaries, sexual boundaries. I could almost just flip sort of back and forth from being a person who had absolutely no boundaries—and therefore no con-science."

Despite what happened to her, Sandi remains puzzled why a woman like herself, who grew up in the church, was unable to determine the difference between right and wrong and to recognize the need to establish boundaries.

"But back then I just couldn't think clearly. I knew I was probably headed for a nervous breakdown. I was vulnerable to anyone who wanted to come into my life."

She remembers becoming intimately involved with her present husband, Don Peslis, while waiting for her divorce to be finalized. Don was a member of her band at the time and also was married.

"We began what in our hearts felt like a new and fresh friendship," she recently told a magazine interviewer. "We knew we loved each other very much and that continued to grow."

Looking back, Sandy today admits that regardless of how

the two of them felt about each other, what she did was inappropriate behavior for a Christian.

"I had an affair and that was wrong," she states unequivocally. "I was not honest about it, and that was wrong. I made decisions and choices that greatly hurt the name of the Lord and the cause of His people."

When word of the affair eventually leaked out to the media, Sandi, who by then was already undergoing spiritual counseling, was devastated. She reacted by publicly admitting her mistake and begging forgiveness from her disappointed fans.

She further recollects turning to prayer, close friends, and scripture to help comfort her though this bleak period of her life.

"I surrounded myself with people who appropriately extended the hand of mercy," she submits. "These were people who no matter what I needed would not walk out of my life—people who were there to help me put my life back together.

"Reading scripture was also very important to me—particularly John 8. I kind of found it in high school when I was doing Bible study. It's a very powerful scripture and it helped me through all of this. There's live truth packed in scripture and a lot of wisdom in scripture—basic good, moral principles."

Today Sandi is able to see that the public exposure of her affair had some benefit, because it gave her the opportunity to confess her sins.

"As embarrassing and humiliating as it was, when I acknowledged the truth first with myself, then with my pastor, my church family, and with the people I individually needed to go to and ask forgiveness, there was also something quite freeing about doing that," she declares.

"There's a lot of freedom found in acknowledging and handing over the truth to the Lord. My commitment was to be honest and be held accountable. I knew I was dealing a little bit with the dark side of the truth right now, but that there would be a freedom and a release that came—there would be hope on the other side of devastation."

For those who may be involved in an extramarital affair, Sandi counsels that they confront the truth about the type of life they are leading. "As quickly as you are able to do so, don't minimize the truth," she counsels. "Don't deny the truth of what you're doing or hold back pieces of it. That will help your healing come so much quicker.

"Read John's words and acknowledge the truth. Go to church, and don't be afraid to surround yourself with people who will reflect the honest truth back to you. Just know that God forgives your sins and that he loves you. . . ."

Bruce Carroll

And we know that all things work together for good to them that love God, to them who are the called according to his purpose.

ROMANS 8:28

WHEN TWO-TIME GRAMMY WINNER Bruce Carroll looks into a mirror, what he says he sometimes sees gazing back at him is the reflection of a man who has had a "lifetime of falling down and getting up."

It seems an apt description of this award-winning contemporary Christian music superstar who, despite having contended with some difficult times—including struggles with alcohol and drug addiction—has always managed to get back on his feet.

Still another severe blow knocked the six-time Dove nominee to his feet—learning that his wife had cancer.

It was during this anxious period of his life that the forty-three-year-old San Antonio native, who in 1997 was voted Favorite Country Artist by readers of *CCM Magazine*, discovered the verse from Romans 8: 28.

He credits that scripture not only for supporting him through those trying days but for bringing him even closer to his wife, and the Lord, as well.

"I believe in those words absolutely," he testifies. "There's a lot of promise and hope in them."

IT'S BEEN A BUMPY ROAD FOR BRUCE CARROLL, a talented singer and songwriter with a Texas-flavored folk music style who is not afraid to express through his music all the trials and tribulations he has encountered along the way.

But there's more than just gritty reality to his lyrics—Bruce's music also offers a positive message of God's love, grace, and protection no matter what peril may be encountered on life's journey.

In fact, if there is one theme that permeates much of his songwriting, it is about how God more often than not reveals Himself during times of personal crises rather than when life is going well—a philosophy that Bruce honed when Nikki, his wife of more than eighteen years, faced cancer surgery.

The voice of the soft-spoken Texan still brims with emotion when he recalls those harrowing days.

"It was about five years ago and my wife had a real bad case of cancer. And I just really stood on that verse, you know, like Lord, I don't know why this is happening and it doesn't seem very fair. And I could lose my wife over this. But I'm just going to believe that somehow this is good for us and that it's going to work together for our good and for your glory."

Bruce still recollects his feelings of helplessness and how he decided to step out into faith as a way of coping with those feelings. "The stress was so high and things so weird that all I could do was step out in faith and just hang on to that verse. I just kept saying that even though I didn't understand why this was happening, I knew that it would somehow be okay.

"And I knew that while I might not know for a long time why this was happening, that God would ultimately one day reveal to me why this took place. I also knew that He loves to take dark and dismal things and turn them around for our good and His glory.

"I believed that if I was just patient and just hung on and stepped out in faith—you know, as the Lord says, 'walk by faith, not by sight'—that He was in control and would reveal these things to me."

Bruce's faith in the Lord was rewarded. Not only was the surgery successful, but he also walked away from that experience stronger in his marriage and faith than ever before.

"They were able to get all of the cancer. And in the process—you know, going through that—it caused me to deal with a lot of things. It forced me to reassess the relationship that I was having with my wife. It brought us closer together as a family. It brought us closer together as a man and his wife.

"So in many ways what happened was God's way of bringing us closer together as a family. That's what I think it was all about. It really impacted our lives for the good.

"And in the midst of it, God also showed what He's able to do and how powerful He is and how He can do anything that He wants to. And he chose to heal her, so you know, it was a cool thing."

Today Bruce is a contented man with a passion for religion. He even describes his career as a "musical ministry." His music gives him an opportunity to share God's word outside Christian circles, but Bruce adds that he does so "without beating people over the head."

His newfound love of religion also extends beyond the concert arena. Almost any Tuesday night Bruce can be found at a men's Bible study group near Hendersonville, Tennessee, where he, his wife, and six children live. He is also active with a humanitarian organization known as Mercy Ministries.

But Bruce's life hasn't always been such a contented, God-filled one as it is today. For more years than he cares to admit, Bruce descended into the abyss of alcohol and drug abuse—once nearly losing his life as a result of an overdose.

The oldest of four siblings, Bruce speculates that one reason why he fell prey to chemical addiction is because "I came from a broken-home situation. I remember at a very early age going to church, but after Mom and Dad split up, we didn't go at all. I was about ten when that happened. And after that I didn't have much of a religious grounding.

"The whole spiritual aspect really didn't start creeping in until I was in my teens. Then I started to ask all the big questions like 'Whoa, how did all this get here?' I was starting to search for my spiritual significance, but I was also into drugs a lot and was drinking a lot."

Meanwhile, Bruce continued to pursue his dream of becoming a professional musician. "I've always loved music—I've always had a passion for playing and singing," he asserts. "Everyone in our family has this God-given musical bent."

At age ten, Bruce was already singing in public, and he was performing professionally at fifteen. When in his twenties, he could be found plying his acoustic style of music in clubs and bars throughout the state.

While Bruce's reputation as a talented performer was growing quickly, so was his addiction to alcohol and drugs. "I was really an out-of-control guy with any kind of substance," he reflects. "I guess I was really searching for my own inner being in a reckless kind of way."

After nearly losing his life in a drug overdose, Bruce believes that God stepped in to save him. His "angel" came in the guise of Bruce's older brother, Milton, formerly a country music performer and today a pastor in Boulder, Colorado.

"He used to be like me," Bruce recollects. "In fact, I was striving to be just like him. He was a great singer and a great player and had made a couple of records on his own in the early 1970s. He was out on the road touring with people like Michael Martin Murphy and Jerry Jeff Walker—that country crowd at the time.

"And I was striving to do the record thing and become a big star and do just that kind of thing. I was doing it on a much smaller scale. And both of us were like heavily into the drug scene. We'd have a great time together. We'd get drunk together and do dope together and get thrown in jail together several times. And he was just a guy that I really patterned myself after."

But in 1978 things changed for Milton when he discovered the Lord. "He got saved and embraced Christianity. It totally changed him in a major radical way. He was now so radically different from who he had been that it really weirded me out. It was really confounding to me. I couldn't figure out what he was up to with this Christianity."

Milton then decided it was time for Bruce to change, as well. "Over the next year or so he just really went on this mission to get me saved," Bruce recalls. "He would speak the Word to me from time to time—he even sent me a Bible with my name on it. He would call me a lot and read me scriptures. He would call, read me a scripture, call back later and read me another scripture.

"It was weird, but those scriptures were important in changing me. And I saw how different he was, too. I saw that he did have real peace and this real calm and stillness about himself, which is something he never had before."

Gradually Bruce's resistance to his brother's ministering

began to lessen. "I was twenty-four or twenty-five years old at the time, and I felt that my life was a mess. I was in financial ruin, and I had a lot of pressures on my life. I had come to the end of myself. I was really out of control.

"I began to see the possibilities that my brother talked about. I had always deep inside been seeking that kind of peace. It really impacted on me how a transformation could take place in the life of somebody so quickly and sincerely.

"It wasn't phony. Man, he was just passionately in love with the Lord, and it showed. So God just really in a mighty way used him and the scriptures to bring me to a place of brokeness in 1979.

"And also when I was coming to the end of myself I would hearken back to those scriptures that he would quote to me—like how I could be a new creation. How I could have peace and victory and all these things that he said I could have and that he was exhibiting in his own life. It was pretty amazing how much power there was in the hearing of those scriptures."

Bruce recalls taking his first step toward recovery by making a decision to give up alcohol and drugs. Next he joined a twelve-step program. "By now I had been sober for a while, but I still went to get some help and was working the twelve-step plan.

"It really caused me to have to look inside myself. I had

to ask the tough questions without being able to escape with booze or drugs. It all worked together, and then, in 1979, I gave my heart to the Lord."

That same year Bruce gave his music to the Lord, as well.

He recalls no longer being interested in pursuing a secular career as a singer and songwriter. Instead, what Bruce now wanted most was to sing God-inspired music.

"I was a new believer, and I was yearning for someone to tell me that they knew how I felt—so alone and isolated, paying the price for sins I had committed. I had never heard songs about life issues like struggling with your humanity. That's why I started writing those songs."

Bruce decided to take off for Nashville with nothing more than "faith and a pocketful of his new songs;" eventually he was discovered there by Word Records. The Christian music charts tell the rest of the story.

Today, despite his busy schedule, Bruce submits that he always finds time each day to read scripture or involve himself in some other form of worship. "It's a pretty full life these days, thanks to God's blessings," he declares. "I just want to keep being thankful and ask Him to keep me balanced as I walk.

"Every day I spend fifteen minutes—sometimes longer—on the verse from Romans. It's my most favorite scripture because it's manifested itself in my life so many times—particularly during hard times.

"And I talk to the Lord all the time as I would to my father. There are times when I'll feel real reverent and I'll feel the need to be a little bit more ceremonial. That's when I get on my knees and just really start praising Him and thanking Him. But I mostly just talk to Him all day. I feel that He's always with me and He's right here."

As someone who has had his share of life's ups and downs, Bruce counsels anyone facing difficult times to read his favorite scripture. "Chew on it if you're troubled or down and out," he advises. "There's a lot of depth in that and a lot of promise and a lot of hope. Read it and believe it and know that He will make things work out for the good."

Bryan Duncan

ASK FIVE-TIME DOVE-NOMINATED singer and songwriter Bryan Duncan for his favorite scripture, and the son of a hellfire-and-brimstone Pentecostal preacherman politely declines to offer one.

For anyone who is at all familiar with this complex, sometimes brooding, Christian-music perennial's life, who persisted in his passion for music despite objections from his parents and church members, such a response is not really a surprising one.

The Utah native submits that he still feels wounded by memories of how scripture was quoted in an attempt to discourage his interest in music, which is why he continues to have a difficult time quoting it in public.

"I can't throw scripture at people and tell them how things should be done," he declares. "Those words are divinely inspired, and I'm grateful when I hear the truth in scriptures. But a lot of times people say things using scripture that are not based on love, but hate.

"That's probably why I don't share my favorite scripture with too many people. Growing up I've seen the Bible used so much to manipulate people, and a lot of it was used to tear me down. It's hard to remove that mental recording. . . ."

BRYAN DUNCAN BELIEVES IT'S ALL RIGHT TO develop a slow and steady relationship with God—as he has done rather painfully over the years. In fact, the title of one of his earlier best-selling albums, *Slow Revival*, reflects just that sentiment.

"People just have to understand that even though they might not be where they would like to be in their spirituality, they should not be discouraged and give up," he asserts. "You have to take courage in your shortcomings and remember that God loves you unconditionally."

It's advice that comes straight from the heart, because getting to the point of his current spiritual walk has been—and continues to be—a slow and deliberate process for the forty-four-year-old Christian music artist.

"My story is different," the blond performer declares. "It's absolutely backward from most people. I was raised in church from day one. I was in church before I was a week old."

Bryan relates that his father was the pastor of the local Pentecostal church and his mother was the church organist. He recalls growing up with a stern, fundamentalist brand of religion, one that he admits sometimes made him feel "trapped."

"It was a very strict religious upbringing—although, you know, as a kid you wouldn't know strict from a hole in the wall," he submits. "That's just the way it was. My parents weren't really oppressive, but they were workaholics and they didn't communicate very much with us kids.

"My dad was a preacher and he did well on the pulpit, but off the stage he was exactly as I'm turning out—I write songs well and I communicate songs well on the stage, but I still have no clue how to talk to people most of the time offstage. And my dad's pretty much the same way. There's an emotional vacancy that I grew up with.

"And my mom, she went through a lot of hard things, but she's very quiet. There they were ministers in an emotional church, but that's the only place that they were really emotional. Otherwise they were really on the stoic side. They were really fun people, but they couldn't communicate emotionally with their children."

It was in this type of family environment—one replete with many stringent rules but little flexibility—that sixteen-year-old Bryan began to rebel. It wasn't drugs or alcohol that he turned to, but music—a form of expression that was not in great favor among his parents and church members.

Bryan, however, viewed the matter a bit differently. "Music was probably my saving grace over the years," he declares. "It was a way of expressing my frustrations about being trapped. If I was angry I could play rock and roll. That certainly expressed anger better than anything else. So it became a kind of salvation for me—a way for me to sort things out."

His passion for music got an unexpected boost as a result of a gift he received from one of the more sympathetic church members. "A lady in our church gave me a guitar that belonged to her son who was my age but committed suicide. Looking back on it, it's like the Lord took something tragic and made it something else."

Music served another function in his life, he recalls. It enabled Bryan to cope with the loneliness he often experienced as a result of traveling about the country with his Bible-preaching parents.

"We moved around a lot. Me and my two brothers and one sister grew up all over the place. I was born in Ogden, but we lived in Washington State, and North Carolina was where we eventually stayed a lot.

"So I was always the new kid in school or the visitor to a church. I learned pretty quickly just to keep to myself. I don't think I was very outgoing whatsoever all the way through high school.

"And because of our religion, too—you didn't smoke, you didn't dance, you didn't cuss, and you didn't chew—I think I was like a kind of an oddity to the other students. They figured I was too good for everybody else.

"Of course, I never felt that way, but it certainly closed me up. Until I started writing songs I had no outlet. And I imagine that without music I would have been more self-destructive earlier on in my life."

Although he enjoyed music, Bryan remembers not considering it as a professional career. Instead, in 1972 he enrolled at Southeastern Bible College in Lakeland, Florida.

It was there that Bryan—who was always seen around campus playing his favorite guitar—was encouraged by a friend to pursue music as more than just a hobby. Taking his friend's advice, the twenty-year-old ministry student formed the Sweet Comfort Band, and some of his shyness began to melt away.

"I was learning how to be more sociable—especially with girls, because they liked the way I could play guitar." He chuckles. "They didn't mind being sung to. I would just carry a guitar around my back and play songs everywhere."

But, again, Bryan found himself in a clash with religious authority. College administrators had decided that the long-haired, guitar-playing Bible student was not quite the image the college wanted to project. So Bryan was asked to leave. "It was my nonconformity. My refusal to follow the rules," he asserts.

For Bryan, his expulsion from college reopened old wounds. "It was always a matter of performance growing up in church," he submits. "If you led song services and stuff you were cool, but if you hung out in the back of the church afterward and smoked cigarettes, you weren't cool.

"It was a very conditional love and it would make me angry. I would hear all the time that 'God loves you unconditionally.' But, at the same time, if you looked a certain way or didn't live up to certain expectations—like at college— then they didn't love you that much. There wasn't really an example of unconditional love. I'd never experienced real examples of unconditional love."

Which brings Bryan back to why he is reluctant to offer his favorite scripture, although he has many.

"In growing up I've just seen the Bible being used to manipulate people so much," he asserts. "And I've seen so much misuse of the terminology and the words. And so much of the scripture was handed to me in ways that made me feel worse about my situation. A lot of times people used scripture to tear me down because they saw me as being arrogant.

"But if you're really not arrogant, and what you're suffering from is low self-esteem—like I was—and when they start sharing scriptures about 'what you ought to be doing' or 'the right thing to do,' when they start throwing that at you—it's like prescribing the wrong medication. That's part of the problem. A lot of scripture is misused to tear people down. I still suffer from a lot of the aftereffects of that."

Although Bryan admits he sometimes finds himself still "wincing" at certain scriptures that conjure up bad memories for him, he remains appreciative of God's holy words. But, he adds, he will only read and share scripture in a group situation where discussion accompanies the readings.

"I like to go over it with other people because I still remember some of the negative effects it's had on me. And every once in a while I come across scripture and I think, 'You know what? That's pretty good.' There are a lot of scriptures I feel that way about. But I'm not throwing them at people and saying how things should be done."

While Bryan admits he is far from the spiritual closeness with God that he desires, the award-winning singer and songwriter feels satisfied that his "slow revival" is progressing at its own steady pace.

"I always talk about my relationship with the Lord through the aspect of how far I feel from Him most of the time. A lot of my songs are about the distance between me and Him, or the desire to be closer to Him.

"I know I haven't arrived spiritually yet, but I'm okay where I'm at. God still loves me in my failures or in my struggle to achieve something that I don't have now. And that's a very good place to be.

"I'm also amazed at how patient God has been with me in the face of some of the things I've said. That's why more than anything else I still cling to Him. He has been more patient and long-suffering than any person I know."

Despite his particular relationship with scripture, Bryan does not hesitate to recommend anyone struggling with a problem to turn to it for comfort.

"I think that reading scripture for many people would be helpful—it just has to do with how you were raised," he offers. "Jesus talks about listening and hearing if you have ears to hear, and you have to try to hear the scriptures in a way that's not distorted. Not everyone hears scripture the way I do, because a lot of it was quoted to me in hatred and anger.

"But I also accept that these words are divinely inspired and have survived a long time. To turn back to a Bible from the fifteenth century and see pretty much the same text as we read today is pretty impressive.

"That's why I think meditating on scripture is powerful. It helps to make sure that you're getting the right message from what's being said. It's also important to have some loving context before you start."

He further suggests getting involved with some support group in dealing with personal issues. " 'Forsake not the gathering together,' " he quotes from scripture. "Fellowship with honest believers in the sense of community has probably been one of the most important things in my own life.

"It helped to be able to talk through stuff with others to make them understand how angry I was about how religion was handed to me. It would have been hard for me to turn to the scriptures until I got that taken care of."

Carolyn Arends

*Delight thyself also in the Lord; And He shall
give thee the desires of thine Heart.*

PSALM 37:4

REFLECTING UPON THE ROAD SHE'S traveled, singer and songwriter Carolyn Arends believes she might not have been able to navigate some of its unexpected twists and turns were it not for the inspiration she received from Psalm 37.

The gifted twenty-eight-year-old Canadian native, who is best known for her thoughtful lyrics and smooth and soaring vocals, credits this verse for helping her to cope with many of life's detours—including a failed high school romance and a confusing period of her life when she was unable to decide whether she wanted to pursue a singing career.

Even today the 1995 Dove Award-winning Reunion Records star, who has registered high marks on the Canadian pop scene as well as on Christian radio charts, confides that she often turns to this scripture when she is feeling anxious or uncertain.

"It's the Word and my relationship with God that renews me," Carolyn professes. "It allows me to be quite often a very happy person or, at least, a hopeful person. This scripture changes the world from being me-centered to being God-centered. It gives me an awareness that He's here, and He's loving me."

———

BORN AND RAISED IN VANCOUVER, BRITISH COL-
umbia, where she was the oldest of three children, Carolyn's
passion for music dates back to a very early age.

She recalls a childhood singing in Baptist churches in Brit-
ish Columbia's Lower Mainland with her musically talented
family. Another memory is "riding around in my parents' car
picking out harmony parts from Bill and Gloria Gaither rec-
ords."

The accomplished, red-haired artist even jokes about her
early love for music. "My mom claims that as soon as I could
talk I would sing myself to sleep. It wouldn't make sense,
but it would rhyme!"

Carolyn's parents, recognizing their young daughter's
budding talent, purchased her first guitar. Guitar lessons were
followed by piano lessons. Carolyn remembers repaying that
debt at age nine by writing a song for Mother's Day. "Then
I wrote an ecology-type song for my fourth-grade class and
songs just started pouring out of me."

The attractive green-eyed entertainer describes her home
life as one filled with religion as well as music. Carolyn's
father, a banker, was also the church organist, while her
mother, a nurse, served as the children's choir director.

"I was raised in a home where faith was central," Carolyn
offers. "I think I was really fortunate, because a lot of people
are raised in religious homes and religion turns them off. But

my parents' relationship with God was a living, breathing thing, and I remember embracing Christianity very early—I was four years old."

She chuckles at that memory. "I approached my parents and said, 'I want to become a Christian. What is that?' I'm twenty-eight now and that was twenty-four years ago. And I can't really say that there's ever been a time since then when I haven't believed."

Although she continued to write songs throughout her teenage years, Carolyn recollects that a musical career was not her first choice.

"I believed that I had to do something sensible. I thought I'd be a doctor, so I went to the university on a bio-chem scholarship. After a year, I discovered I didn't like the smell of formaldehyde," she says with a laugh.

"I really was in the piano rooms writing songs more than I was doing anything else, including going to class. I think God planned it that way to redirect my life appropriately. It became apparent that music was something God had seriously laid on my heart."

After switching her major to liberal arts, Carolyn met Mark, a young college athlete and her future husband-to-be. It was Mark who encouraged Carolyn to pursue her love of music and even managed to get one of her demo tapes to the late, great songwriter Mark Heard.

Heard was impressed enough by what he heard to give the young songwriter's career a push in the right direction, and Carolyn eventually found herself working as a staff songwriter at Benson Music.

It was while writing heartfelt songs for Christian artists like Michael James, 4Him, Susan Ashton, and others that Carolyn began to perform on her own in clubs in her hometown of Vancouver.

"I began to realize that the artist thing—performing— was part of what God had in mind for me. He could use my talent to do good and I loved it. There's nothing like the connection music gives between people."

Still, she remembers hesitating to take the plunge as a full-time performer. Uncertain about what to do, Carolyn recollects turning to her Bible and Psalm 37. Once before in her life that verse had helped her to cope with a confusing situation.

"I was sixteen and in the eleventh grade when I had a traumatic thing happen with my boyfriend," she recalls. "I was really taken with him and we ended up breaking up. It was a hard thing at that time. My youth counselor's wife gave me that verse and it helped me get through that. And I've come back to it and back to it."

Now, as she pondered whether to leave her job as a songwriter and embark on a solo singing career, Carolyn again turned to her favorite scripture.

"This verse helped me again. I thought that writing songs was all I wanted to do. I was actually kind of shy and I just didn't know if the performing thing was what I wanted.

"And I think I also know so many talented people that would love to be singing and writing professionally and it never happened to them. So I was really wary of wanting that—I was just sort of aware of the odds. I really struggled with even letting myself sort of dream of such a thing."

But Carolyn remembers how the verse seemed to speak directly to her. "It reminded me to delight myself in the Lord, and an answer was certain to follow. I said, 'Okay, maybe God is trying to tell me something.' I sort of surrendered myself to that.

"When you're trying to determine God's will for your life, there are many things that are a given. We know, for example, that it is God's will for us to become more like Christ.

"But in terms of what doors to walk through and what to pursue, I really learned from that verse that the emphasis should be in delighting ourselves in the Lord.

"Instead of trying to sit around and figure out what He has in store for us, we should figure out who He is and delight in that. We should value the things that He values and invest ourselves in knowing Him.

"And what you discover is that it's not so much that He gives you what you wanted previously but that He changes what you want. He gives your heart the desires that will make you more like Him. And music is an opportunity to forge a connection to Him."

Carolyn decided to take the plunge and perform solo, a career move that quickly resulted in a 1995 debut album and accolades that proclaimed her one of Canada's great new pop finds.

Today Carolyn gives much credit to her favorite scripture for encouraging her to step out in faith. "That scripture is one that's very much hidden in my heart," she asserts. "It just sort of comes up for me anytime I'm ever trying to evaluate what to do next. It's pretty ingrained in me at this point."

She adds that all scripture is filled with encouragement and life-affirming power. "They're God-breathed words," she proclaims. "If we commit ourselves to holding the words of the Bible in our hearts, the Holy Spirit will use that to change us.

"Maybe that's our part of the deal—to apply ourselves to knowing scripture. If we actually learn the words and commit them to memory, then the Holy Spirit takes that and changes us."

Prayer is also an "ongoing thing" in her life, she offers. "I'm on tour now and our band usually goes onstage seven-thirty every night. So pretty much you'll always find us around seven-ten or seven-fifteen praying as a band. That's something we definitely do before we do a show.

"I'm trying to learn how to pray without ceasing—it's something the Bible tells us to do. It's basically being in dialogue with God all day long. And then there's my formal times of prayer. I set aside this time to communicate with God. But I pretty much pray at any time and keep that dialogue open."

Although she works hard at it, Carolyn admits that her spiritual life is far from perfect. There have been times, she recalls, when she has felt discouraged and struggled to keep her faith intact.

But she does not chastise herself for such doubtful moments. "From all my experiences, my personal conviction is that the deeper the faith, the greater the doubt. It's like the more you go into the mystery of God, the more He is mysterious.

"If He really is infinite and we really are finite, there are going to be things about this relationship that are very frustrating and very hard to understand. It's like the higher the peak you go to, the more the valley.

"I'm at my core a believer. I sometimes have a lot of questions, but I can't help know that in the depths of my being I believe in God and that He knows me and loves me."

Geoff Moore

Seeing then that we have a great high priest, that is passed into the heavens, Jesus the Son of God, let us hold fast our profession.

For we have not a high priest which cannot be touched with the feelings of our infirmities; but was in all points tempted like as we are, yet without sin.

Let us therefore come boldly unto the throne of grace, that we may obtain mercy, and find grace to help in time of need.

HEBREWS 4:14–16

GEOFF MOORE STILL CAN CLEARLY recall his time of need—the mournful period following his father's fatal heart attack—and the grace he found afterward.

The veteran frontman for Geoff Moore and the Distance, a dynamic Grammy and Dove award-winning pop/blues/rock band, had just turned nineteen at the time of his father's death.

It was during this "season of the wilderness" that Geoff, considered to be one of Christian music's premier rockers, affirms that he came to understand the meaning of the phrase "a man of sorrows."

But the 1993 Grammy Award winner submits that it was also an experience from which he emerged with a clearer understanding of the meaning of faith. And he gives much credit for that feeling to a reading of the scripture from Hebrews.

"On a day-to-day basis this scripture has been a real source of strength to me," declares the Michigan native, whose group was voted Favorite Pop Group in a 1997 poll of readers of *CCM Magazine*.

"It has always served to remind me that I am never alone—despite what Satan would try to have us think. In all my struggles, no matter how distant I may feel from God, it reminds me that not only is He one of our high priests but that He has always been one of us, and that's comforting for me to know."

GEOFF MOORE, THEN A NINETEEN-YEAR-OLD college sophomore, will never forget that Good Friday when his father, fifty-nine-year-old Grafton Moore, succumbed to a heart attack.

"It was his second heart attack," Geoff recollects. "He had had a first one two years earlier on another Good Friday when we were playing tennis together. He was a fiercely competitive guy."

Geoff remembers being at his fiancée's home in Chicago when he learned the shocking news and the profound affect that phone call had on his life.

"I had lived a very grief-free life until that point," Geoff relates. "My father's funeral was the first funeral I had ever attended. It was my first journey through a really lonely place."

The memory of that loneliness still haunts him. Today the easygoing, blond musician concludes that Satan often uses such feelings to try to separate people from God.

"I think one of the major attacks Satan puts on mankind is the whole area of isolation," he reflects. "If you look at men and women who have stumbled in their faith, isolation is often a common element—not necessarily being alone as far as being alone in numbers, but being alone in the area of accountability and in relationship to God."

Geoff recalls that one tool which eventually helped him surmount his loneliness was a reading of scripture from Hebrews. He says it served to remind him that the Lord is always available for support and comfort.

"We are never alone, regardless of our struggles," Geoff professes. "Nothing can separate us from the love of God no matter how distant we may feel from Him. So we have nothing to hide, lose, fear, or ever prove. God's love saved us from sin, so it can—and will—rescue us from our daily trials, as well."

The popular artist turns back the pages to the years when he and his father shared the good life together. "We had a great relationship," he recalls with a smile. "It was just as good as a father and son could hope to be."

His soft-spoken voice continues to register delight as he recalls those days and his years growing up in southern Michigan agricultural communities like Holly and Ortonville.

"My dad was a retired steel worker," he relates. "He owned a small steel fabricating business and sold goods to Detroit's auto industry. Our family name was on the sign outside the business." Geoff describes his mother as a "homebody" who was kept busy raising her large family.

The youngest of four children, Geoff offers that he can

remember many times when his family was short on cash, but never were they short of love for each other or God. "We came out of real poverty—that kind of environment," he declares. "It served as a great palette me to write about later as an artist and songwriter.

"My mom and dad were not Christians when they were married, but they became Christians before I was born. So I was raised in kind of a first-generation Christian home. It was a healthy, well-balanced home with a real understanding of what it is to live a life of grace."

Geoff goes on to recall how, during his high school and college years, he would work side by side with his father after school, on weekends, and during the summer months.

"It's the only job I ever had. It's all I ever planned to do," he asserts. "I got married when I got out of college and started working there. My dad—when he was still alive—believed that you should start working at the bottom, so I did all kinds of stuff—I was a shop foreman, a welder—almost anything he wanted me to do no matter how hard or lousy the work was."

It was after his father's death that Geoff's passion for carrying on with the family business was replaced by a growing interest in performing music. "I just began to lose my fire for it. Now I wanted to see where music would take me."

Geoff remembers beginning to "dabble some with Christian music" while attending Taylor University in Upland, Indiana. "We played youth ministry kinds of things—that kind of stuff." At one point during his senior year, Geoff and some friends even made a trip to Nashville, where they recorded a demo, although nothing ever came of it.

His growing interest in music was not received with much enthusiasm at home, he recollects. "It was almost an artless home unless you consider a great pass play, a great curve ball, or a great fly-fishing cast as art." Geoff chuckles. "It was definitely a sporting home. My dad had even played some professional farm club baseball."

Geoff submits that he enjoyed listening to rock music, although he had some problems with its lyrics. "It didn't represent who I wanted to be," he declares.

In Christian music, however, the young musician found both a sound and a style of writing that he could relate to. "It really filled that void. So that's where my interest in it started. And then I began playing with this band at Taylor, but that was a part-time thing."

All of the teenager's plans came to a screeching halt upon his father's death. There are still traces of emotion etched in his voice as he recalls those sorrowful days.

"It was one of the most difficult times in my life—it was terrible and frightening," he submits. "I remember after I got that call, I put down the phone and said to myself, 'I'm really going to find out if my faith is a real part of my life.' It really became one of the most defining moments in my walk with Christ.

"I also learned a great lesson that for whatever reason I hadn't learned until that point—that the closer a relationship is, the easier it is to deal with loss. I'd always thought that if I'm really close to this person, it's going to be even harder to deal with it if they're taken away by death.

"But I learned that just the opposite is true. Having regret that you weren't close is even worse. The more resolved our lives are in relationship to each other, the more it prepares us to continue to live on without each other. That's why it's important to say what you need to say and communicate your feelings."

Geoff describes his life following his father's funeral as a "season of wilderness." He recalls feeling very much alone but not alienated from God. "I hadn't lost my faith—I hadn't walked away from God—but I was going through a time when I was feeling vulnerable."

Geoff credits scripture for helping to renew him and turning personal tragedy into a powerful life-affirming lesson.

"Scripture gave me a great sense of God's purpose in life. It was like I became wildly sensitized to the spiritual word," he recollects. "Up until that point there was just this feeling that the world and its pursuits were completely insignificant. Reading scripture made me feel like I belonged to the world, again. I've tried to hold on to that feeling because I was as spiritually keen as I ever might be again in my life."

Which is why the Christian music superstar encourages anyone who has experienced the loss of a loved one also to turn to scripture for strength and comfort.

"Scripture taught me that as we face death, we come to the single greatest moment of what all of Christ's sacrifice was pointing to. It was to bring eternal life. And so, for me, there was an enormous feeling of completion in regard to my father's life. The man for so many years had led this faithful walk. He had lived well, he died well, and he lived life in the light of the eternal."

Geoff also counsels mourners to express their grief fully. "I didn't hold back at all. I really went through a physical side of grieving that I found to be fundamental in getting to the place I feel that God wanted me to be.

"So I would encourage people to do that. If it's screaming, yelling, crying, running—whatever—the idea is to let God take us through that and then let it go. There's just too many cultural boundaries about how we should behave in such circumstances.

"The way I grieved became an enormous opportunity for me in the area of evangelism for people to watch me and my family go through this period of loss. The thing that drew people in was the fact that there was pain, that there was sorrow, and that there was brokeness.

"But in the midst of it there was peace that passes understanding. There was a sense of purpose, a sense of closure, and at the same time a sense of beginning and rebirth."

Besides a regular reading of scripture, Geoff, who today lives in Nashville with his wife and two children, affirms that he leads an active prayer life.

"We have this concept today that we can just pray within the context of our day-to-day lives—that we can pray on the way to work, or on the way home, or in the shower," the Christian music superstar proclaims.

"But that certainly isn't enough. A healthy prayer life requires solitude, isolation—these are the things that I'm trying to pursue, although it doesn't happen often enough.

"My prayer life also revolves around my children and my wife. I feel a real calling and responsibility to intercede on behalf of my kids. I've been entrusted with more than just feeding and clothing these two boys. The same with my marriage. So much of my prayer life is spent when my three family members are asleep. I pray for my family a lot during that time."

John Schlitt

But speaking the truth in love, may grow up into him in all things, which is the head, even Christ:

From whom the whole body fitly joined together and compacted by that which every joint supplieth, according to the effectual working in the measure of every part, maketh increase of the body unto the edifying of itself in love.

EPHESIANS 4:15-16

WITH A GOLD ALBUM, TWO GRAMMY Awards, and multiple Dove Awards to his credit, it is difficult to think of someone as successful as John Schlitt, lead singer of Petra, one of Christian music's legendary rock bands, having once been on the verge of suicide.

But in 1980, with his drug and alcohol problem escalating out of control, the forty-six-year-old music industry veteran, who, in 1997, was voted Favorite Male Vocalist by readers of *CCM Magazine*, recalls how close he was to taking that drastic action.

It would take a reluctantly agreed upon meeting with his wife's pastor to change the mind of the Illinois native, who describes that session as being like someone "hit me over the head with a boulder."

Today the clean and sober Christian rock star no longer thinks of himself as a "lost soul."

Instead, the award-winning singer and songwriter with one of the most distinctive voices in the industry today describes himself as "fulfilled" and a "fanatic" for Jesus.

"I'm a heavy-duty Christian," John professes. "It's the Word of God that has made me a winner."

ONE OF JOHN'S EARLIEST MEMORIES OF GROW-ing up in the small, sleepy midwestern town of Mount Pleasant, Illinois, was his struggle to identify what his religion would be. "My mom was Catholic and my dad was Lutheran, so there was quite a battle going on between them as to which religion I should practice," he recalls.

John remembers that a temporary truce was established when his mother turned to him one day and suggested that he need not attend any church until deciding for himself which religion he wanted to follow.

"Well, after getting that kind of freedom, I didn't go to any church for many, many years—except maybe on Christmas and Easter," he says with a chuckle. "My parents taught me my moral lessons very well, but it wasn't a strong Jesus background."

Despite this religious void in his life, Petra's intense, long-haired lead singer remembers always having a strong attraction toward the spiritual life. "Even back then I knew that God was God. What I didn't know then was how important Jesus Christ was. At the time, I just figured that there was a God who encompassed everything. And He does. But for me, today, it's more specific than that."

It was music—not religion—that was the constant focus of John's life during his teenage years. He had always fantasized about being a rock-and-roll star, and it wasn't too long before he had formed his own successful band—a group that called itself Head East.

The band's growing success marked the beginning of John's downfall. "It wasn't the music, it was the lifestyle," he offers. "I was drinking, doing drugs—the whole thing—because I was a rocker.

"I had fallen into that routine with Head East and I loved it. I would always lie to myself and tell myself that I wasn't hooked. But it was a lie. I was even living back home when I was getting stoned.

"I was surrounded by my parents and my wife, Dorla's, parents. They were all good role models, but basically I was sneaking around living two lives. During the day I was the fine son and husband, and at night I was getting plowed."

John can recall a period of time in 1980 when he was so distraught about his lifestyle that he thought about taking his life. "It wasn't a good life and it led me to think that maybe I was just better off dead than alive," he submits. "But instead of facing my problem, I was so down and depressed that I went off on a six-month binge from March to August."

There is little doubt in John's mind that he would have taken his life had it not been for Dorla.

"While my life was going down the tubes, my wife had gotten saved and become a Christian. And she kept trying to tell me about Jesus and this new form of worship that she had found.

"And I said to myself, 'Oh my gosh, a Holy Roller. I

can't believe it.' Because back then I thought that anybody who got excited about God had to be a 'holy roller.'

"I had been against her getting saved. I was actually pretty mad when she told me that she had fallen for that stuff. But meanwhile, I was heading for suicide because I was destroying my life."

John can remember reluctantly agreeing to meet his wife's pastor, the Reverend Donna Artbach of the New Wine Fellowship Church in Lincoln, Illinois. That fateful meeting would change his life and mark a spiritual turnabout for the strung-out performer.

"Man, it was the first time that somebody really hit me over the head about Jesus Christ," he recalls of that meeting. "This pastor person got the message right between my eyes, and all of a sudden I was in a corner going 'Whoa!'

"I remember the pastor asking me if I wanted to know Jesus and I said, 'Yes.' I got saved that night. I asked Jesus into my heart and then I also became very religious.

"My lifestyle changed completely. I gave up all my addictions. Nineteen eighty-one was the beginning of a new life for me. I spent three months trying to find a new job and I did. I didn't get discouraged. I was just wondering, 'God, what's going to happen to me?'

"I ended up sweeping floors in a tool and dye factory.

Even though I had graduated with a degree in civil engineering from the University of Illinois, I was very happy with that job—I was starting a new life."

But bigger and better things were on their way for John. His big break came in the form of a telephone call from Bob Hartman, Petra's founding member. It had been five years since Hartman had heard John sing, but the young rocker obviously had left a lasting impression on the band's leader.

"He said, 'John, I have only one question for you. Are you still a Christian?' I laughed and I said, 'A heavy-duty one.' And he said, 'That's all we need to know.' John was soon performing on stage again, but this time his talent was not diluted with alcohol or drugs.

Today John considers his work with Petra as a "musical ministry" that puts him in touch with people throughout the world and helps to change lives. He is also a firm believer in the power of scripture.

"There's a lot of power to be gotten from reading it," he declares. "It's the Word of God. The Bible's not just a history book, it's an instruction manual and it's a way to be a winner."

John submits that his choice of Ephesians 4 as his favorite scripture has more to do with his current incarnation as a "saved soul" than his lost years. "I don't think there's been just one scripture that has guided me through my whole Christian life," he explains, "but I chose this one because it's how I'm feeling right now.

"As Christian entertainers we're in the limelight and we stand as examples of Christianity, both good and bad. And I think we're really called upon to be accountable because we are examples.

"I think this scripture can be a reminder to people that we should express the truth in all things." He laughs. "It doesn't sound like it takes much, but we pretty much buck against that every day. I'm guilty of that, too, but it doesn't make it right.

"If we had the courage to live that Godly kind of life no matter what the circumstances—instead of stretching the truth and exaggerating—we might be surprised at what the results will be."

John advises that readers "try to repeat this scripture every day. Try every day to do the best you can. Try to be as faithful, truthful, and righteous as you possibly can.

"If you can function that way, even though you'll sometimes blow it, you'll still be the light that shines. Just remember that there has never been a perfect human being who has walked this Earth—except for Jesus Christ."

Kathy Troccoli

Then took Mary a pound of ointment of spike-nard, very costly, and anointed the feet of Jesus, and wiped his feet with her hair: and the house was filled with the odor of the ointment.

JOHN 12:3

CHRISTIAN ARTIST KATHY TROC-coli was poised on the verge of stardom in the 1980s when she suddenly decided to take a break from the fast-paced Nashville music scene.

The rising young singer and songwriter had recently become a "committed Christian," and Kathy felt she needed some peace and quiet to reflect upon her spiritual transformation. She was also struggling with a personal problem that she wanted to address—an eating disorder called bulimia.

When Kathy emerged from her six-year hiatus ready to perform again, tragedy struck. The thirty-eight-year-old New York native learned that her mother was diagnosed with cancer.

Although she was prepared to delay her return to the recording studio, her mother insisted otherwise. The result was a hit album, *Sounds of Heaven*, which spawned five number-one singles.

Today Kathy, who has been nominated for multiple Grammy and Dove awards, credits scripture for helping to sustain her during that painful period of her life when she would shuttle between the recording studio and her mother's hospital room.

"I've been continually blessed by that story of Mary at His feet," Kathy proclaims. "Mary knew what God had saved her from. She fell in love with Jesus and knew who He was and who she would be without Him—that He had saved her from so much—just like He's saved me. . . ."

IT WAS 1982, AND TWENTY-TWO-YEAR-OLD RE-union Records recording artist Kathy Troccoli was on the verge of overnight success in the Christian music arena. The attractive, dark-eyed vocalist with the bright smile and heart-felt lyrics was touring with Amy Grant and Michael W. Smith at the time, wowing audiences and garnering several Dove and Grammy nominations along the way.

But despite her quickly developing success, Kathy, who was raised in a close-knit Italian family on Long Island, was gripped by inner turmoil. A few years earlier she had un-dergone a spiritual renewal and became a "committed Chris-tian." But now there were times when she felt that her admiring fans expected too much of her newfound relation-ship with Jesus.

"I was discovered quickly, and after a year and a half I was kind of shipped off to Nashville," she submits. "It was great that I had that opportunity, but then I found myself in this position of ministering, and I wasn't really ready to do that. I was immature as a Christian believer and needed time to work through some of the spiritual issues in my life."

Kathy was also wrestling with another dilemma—the up-

and-coming artist wasn't certain that she wanted to perform only Christian music. She felt keenly attracted to the pop music world, as well.

"I also had a love for music other than gospel music," she recalls, "and I wanted to reevaluate where I was musically. So by the time 1986 came around I had been on the road for about four years, and I felt that I needed a break. I needed to do more soul-searching. I was on the road constantly and I wasn't in a steady fellowship with believers."

Reflecting back on that period, what she recalls seeking most of all was "the sweetness of solitude"—time off so that she could "grow, mature, and heal." In addition, the young star wanted to address a problem that had plagued her for years—bulimia.

"I was obsessed with food," Kathy recollects. "I would gorge myself and then abuse my body with laxatives—even though I was on the thin side. By absorbing food I felt like I was in control and that comforted me. I wanted to deal with that issue as well."

It all added up to leaving the music business for a while. Kathy remembers leaving Nashville and returning home, where she underwent what she describes as a long period of "soul-searching, counsel, and prayer." She adds: "I began to deal with my obsession with food, my relationship toward my mother, and my desire to be a whole, healthy person. I was better able to hear God's voice and understand myself and deal with whatever was in my heart and mind."

By 1991 Kathy recalls feeling full of energy and ready to resume her career. But just as she was getting ready to return to the recording studio, the performer learned of her mother's illness. The news was devastating. Kathy's father had died from colon cancer when she was fifteen, and the thought of losing her surviving parent overwhelmed her.

"When my father died I didn't know as much about Christ then," she relates. "I really didn't enjoy going to church back then. It was a whole different time. I think I was more numb at that time. But with my mother it was different."

Although she had embraced Jesus, Kathy candidly admits that she reacted to the news with rage toward God. "I did shake my fist toward heaven like most people," she discloses. "I remember going into the hospice chapel and I remember lying there and weeping."

But there was a moment that changed her entire attitude—one that Kathy asserts she will never forget. "I was seated alone in the chapel and I heard this gentle voice in my head asking 'Kathy, am I not still God?' And I had to answer that question. Was God still God whether my mother had cancer or not? Were his promises still true? Did it change because my mother had cancer?

"And I remember just weeping, because I couldn't throw away what I had known Jesus to be. That was the turning point for me during that first week. I decided that God is the God of this situation, and someday I'll be able to stand before Him and know all that I need to know about why this happened to my mother—it would all be laid out for me."

Although she still does not comprehend why her mother had to die such a painful death, Kathy has long since reconciled herself with the Lord. "I don't have the answers to all the mysteries of life," she proclaims. "I just know that without Him in my heart I probably would have been a very embittered person.

"I probably would have fed off my own grieving at that time instead of being what my mother needed because of my own self-pity. There was a different hope in my heart because of Jesus.

"My mother's body died that day, but she went from life to life. Did I mourn? Do I miss her? Absolutely. Do I have a grieving like I'll never see her again? I don't have that. I know that my mother is alive in Christ, and that gives me great peace.

"That whole process of her death would have been different without Jesus. For me there's no hope without God. I always want to have that kind of heart. I always want to be aware about who I would be without Christ—that without

Him I would have nothing and that with Him I have every-thing."

Kathy remembers conversations she had with several people at the hospital whose life was not founded on a love for Christ.

"Did I weep like some of those people? Absolutely. But it was a different kind of weeping. I knew where my mother was going. I knew that God had touched her. I knew that He gave me the strength to see life differently. There were people in that hospital that had no hope. And quite frankly, I don't know how people do it without God."

Kathy offers that there was a period of her life when her own heart was not filled with Christ. Although raised as a Roman Catholic and a regular churchgoer with her parents, the Christian music star remembers that there was a lack of intensity in her prayer life.

"Back then, Jesus was just a figure hanging on a cross in church," she submits. "He had no personal connection to me. And religion doesn't bring people much if they don't have a true relationship with God. That's what I was a victim of. I didn't feel a relationship with God and I didn't have one. God was very obscure to me."

It was during the summer of 1978, while at a Long Island community pool where Kathy worked taking memberships, that she became friendly with a girl named Cindy who brought her Bible to the pool with her each day.

Kathy remembers that nothing in her own spiritual life matched the religious fervor expressed by the young woman. "She gave me a Bible to take home and I read it all the way through for the first time. I was nineteen and I wasn't a scripture reader back then. But through the reading of the scriptures I glimpsed a portion of the life of Christ that was totally different than being without Him.

"Then for several months the Holy Spirit was working on my heart. Cindy invited me to her church and I began to change and see things about Jesus like I've never seen them before. I knew that I had to make a choice.

"It wasn't until I took a look at the scriptures and read some of the gospels—especially the Gospel of John—that I came to believe that Jesus was the Son of God, that He lived, died for me, rose again, and everything He said was truth."

Kathy remembers the exact date of her spiritual renewal. "It was on August 5, 1978. Cindy and I prayed with her youth pastor, and it was on that day that I accepted Christ into my heart."

Since then Kathy relates that she has strived to emulate the gospel story of Mary Magdalene at Christ's feet. "I continue to go back to that scripture ever since I truly committed my life to Christ. I oftentimes in prayer and thought want to have that kind of heart—always blessing Him."

Although a devout believer in the power of scripture—

describing it as "the living Word of God"—she cautions that reading scripture is ineffective unless the words of that holy text are read with complete faith.

"You have to believe that scripture is the Word of God, or it won't touch your heart—your heart won't be open to it. That won't happen if you read it with the rationale of the intellect."

For those experiencing the loss of a loved one, Kathy counsels that, in addition to reading scripture, they pause to reflect where their own lives are spiritually. "Who are you placing your trust in? What are you living for? What do you think about life? These are questions you should think about.

"You need to get to a place where you feel that God is as close to you as your very breath. And to do that, all you need to say is 'Come into this situation.' God loves people more than we can ever imagine. It's just that many people don't know that."

As for the future of her own spiritual walk, Kathy proclaims that she hopes to "mature in my faith. I want my life to be about advancing the gospel. I want to live for God in the mundane as much as in front of thousands of people at a concert. I want to continue to have this heart that doesn't rest in the mediocre but is constantly yielding to God."

Larnelle Harris

For God so loved the world, that he gave his only begotten son, that whosoever believeth in him should not perish, but have everlasting life.

JOHN 3:16

AS LARNELLE HARRIS'S CAREER reaches the twenty-five-year milestone, it's no exaggeration to say that this forty-nine-year-old Kentucky native has become an institution in Christian music.

But beyond all the dazzling outward symbols of his successful musical career—including five Grammy Awards, ten Dove Awards, thirteen number-one radio hits, and countless other accolades—what preoccupies this stellar talent the most is how to get people to behave in a manner that is more consistent with Jesus Christ's message of unconditional love.

Having been stung by racism in his own youth, Larnelle has devoted his life to trying to bring about that loving state of mind. He believes this can be accomplished only by a change of heart that comes in part from reading scripture.

"I don't think it's hopeless—I'm not a pessimist," the Brentwood Records superstar affirms. "I believe things can get better. But we need to continually talk about the Lord, talk about model Christianity, talk about unconditional love as best as we can. The answer to fellowship in this world is to model it after the one who practiced it unconditionally."

IN LARNELLE HARRIS'S MORE THAN TWO DEcades of recording, the man and his music have touched the hearts and souls of millions of people around the world.

The tall, intense entertainer has been a featured performer for major events such as the Young Messiah Tour, Promise Keepers conferences, Billy Graham Crusades, and the recent Jerusalem 3000 and Emanuel tours.

Yet Larnelle has not always been impressed by what he has witnessed on those occasions.

"I've always been amazed by the deal that the Lord has given us," he declares, "and that's the opportunity to live it in a kind of utopian situation. And then we go foul that up—just do everything that would disrupt that whole love gift from the Lord."

He cites as an example his recent tour to Jerusalem, where Larnelle states he personally witnessed the strife and hatred between Arabs and Jews. "All those people need to do to start all over again is receive God's love," he offers. "That kind of love is love freely given. There's no reciprocity involved. You don't pay it back. You simply receive it."

Although he believes the solution to such regional strife is a relatively obvious one, Larnelle is enough of a realist to realize how hard it often is for people to grasp that concept. As another example, he cites a trip he made to the former Soviet Union as part of a revival tour.

"We were giving Bibles away, and I remember when we would hand the Bible to some of the folks in the street, in the train stations, and in the hotels, they would automatically try to give them back.

"They either didn't want them—although we gave four million away, so I know they wanted them—or were thinking that if they received something, they would have to pay for it. I guess it's just the way we are. We think if someone does something for us we have to give back down the road. That's just the way we are and this is not how God works."

The legendary singer and songwriter speculates that one reason why many people find it difficult simply to accept God's unconditional love is that so many do not believe they deserve it.

"They think it would be nice to have another chance to correct something that they royally fouled up, but they also believe that their relationship with the Lord is not of the sort that they can receive that gift of unconditional love from Him. Even though God has given us the most precious gift that can be given—Himself—it's just hard for us to receive that gift of love. We feel unworthy of it."

Larnelle remembers learning his own lesson of God's love as a boy growing up in the small farming town of Danville, Kentucky, where he was the youngest of several children.

As a youngster, Larnelle was already taking piano lessons. He also liked to sing, giving his first solo performance at age nine while in church. "I was a boy soprano and I had a kind of unusual voice," he says with a chuckle.

Besides music, Larnelle recollects that at that age God was already within him.

"My mother belonged to the Pentecostal Holiness Church, but I was eleven or twelve years old and going to the Baptist church, because that's where most of my friends were," he recalls. "It wasn't too long before my mom and dad joined this church.

"I was only twelve years old when I decided to become a Christian. And the verse from John was the one that stood out the most for me. It really broke my heart. I couldn't put it together then as well as I can now, but the words had meaning for me. I was amazed that someone could love that much to give His own life.

"I mean, I was taught love by my mom and dad. But being a young Black boy growing up in surroundings that were not always friendly toward Blacks and other minorities, I was subliminally taught to be a little suspicious of other people for my own protection. But Jesus was someone who never did that. He was somebody who really went out of His way not to harbor any ill will—I mean, that really impressed me."

Larnelle confides that while he considers his spiritual walk far from perfect, he tries to the best of his ability to practice

Jesus' brand of unconditional love. "Over the years, I have had—and still have—the responsibility to put myself in a place where God can do His work in my heart," he declares.

"It's only through a change of heart that we can make things like racism go away—it takes a spiritual heart transplant. If things like racism could be done away with by the minds of great men, it would have been done away with already. But it can only be done by putting ourselves in a place where God can teach us the process of love."

Larnelle offers that his favorite scripture helps to get him into that mind-set.

"I think about this scripture a lot," he attests, "because how can you not think about that most basic nugget of the Gospel? For me it's really the basis for everything we believe. It stays with me all the time."

But the "real issue is man's heart," he adds. "It's great and necessary for us to think about this verse and other scripture, and to meet and talk about issues like reconciliation. But how do you really fix something like racism? You have to put yourself in a position where God can change your heart.

"And when you change a man's heart—and only God can do that. That's the business He's in—then all this extra baggage and negativism that we carry around with us at times begins to fade away almost without our knowing."

Larnelle firmly believes it is important to set personal examples of God's love. "It's not the users of the Word, it's the doers that are most effective," he professes. "If I go to witness somebody—let's say he's a non-Christian—and I say, 'You know what, let me show you a couple of things out of the Bible tonight that I've read.'

"And the guy says, 'You know, I don't believe that. I don't believe that Bible. We don't have much to talk about.' Well, then we have to build that relationship so that we can talk about it.

"And the best way I can think about doing that is to display a genuine love in the face of someone who totally disagrees with me. I don't hate them and I don't write them off. I simply continue to love them—because that's what the Bible says we should do. With that kind of example of unconditional love, I think that down the road somewhere I'll get a chance to show that person John 3: 16 and help him understand its meaning."

Larnelle, who today resides in Louisville, Kentucky, with his wife and children, continues to spread his message of love and reconciliation to audiences wherever he travels—from the lawn of the White House to the streets of South Africa and Korea.

"I sing my songs and people just open their hearts. I wouldn't even cross the street to sing a song just for its own sake. I only want to sing songs that change people's lives. I do my best to have fellowship with my Lord because that's where my strength comes from."

Larnelle reveals that despite his busy schedule, he tries to read scripture on a daily basis. "Sometimes I make it and sometimes I don't," he asserts. He offers an anecdote that reflects how imbued he is with scripture.

"I remember that I was sick for some reason and all night these scriptures kept coming to my head. It was like my cup was so full that scripture was spilling out even in my sleep." He chuckles.

Returning to the subject of replacing negative behavior with unconditional love, Larnelle offers these final thoughts:

"It's very simple and it's all based on what I believe. The answer to fellowship in this world is to model ourselves after the one who practiced it unconditionally.

"I honestly believe it's not going to happen through government—through the great minds of men. It will come about as men draw closer to Christ. If I did not believe that, I would not be out here."

Lisa Bragg

Not unto us, O Lord, not unto us, but unto thy name give glory, for thy mercy, and for thy truth's sake.

PSALM 115:1

WHEN FANS APPROACH LISA BRAGG to request an autograph from the twenty-one-year-old lead singer and chief songwriter for Out of Eden, they often get more than they bargained for—Lisa's autograph accompanied by her favorite scripture!

The urban songstress submits that she hopes by doing so her fans will get the point that star worship is not as important as God worship.

"It's my way of saying to people 'Don't look to us, look to the Lord,' " the Ohio native proclaims. "People sometimes forget who gave us this talent and who opened the doors for us and gave us this opportunity."

Lisa, one of three talented sisters who comprise this youthful, Dove award–nominated trio known for its smooth blend of pop and R&B sound, adds that a frequent reading of Psalm 115 also helps to keep her focused on her spiritual walk rather than the group's newfound success.

"If we don't fill our spirit and feed our spirit with the Word of God," the Gotee Records artist declares, "then success is going to be stronger than spirit and that kind of pride is wrong."

THE FUNKY SOUNDS THAT EMERGE FROM OUT OF Eden have as their roots the gospel music that Lisa and her two younger sisters used to sing in church with their mother—a classical pianist—and, sometimes, with their step-father.

Born and raised in Overland, Ohio, Lisa Kimmy Bragg and sisters Andrea, eighteen, and Joy-Danielle, sixteen, developed a passion early in life not only for music but for religion as well.

Raised as a Pentecostal, Lisa remembers "giving my heart to Jesus" at age four. The young star also credits her solid church upbringing for having "a tremendous impact on how we live our lives now."

The attractive twenty-one-year-old with short brown hair and brown eyes also remembers how music was more than just a pastime in her household.

"We used to sing for the fun of it," she chuckles, "but that wasn't good enough for our parents. They really encouraged us to practice and that sort of thing. I was five when I wrote my first song and started singing for people."

When Lisa's mother—musically talented herself—accepted a job with the Fisk University directing the music department's Jubilee Singers, the family relocated to Nashville.

While there, Lisa and her sisters began performing at various talent shows and also worked as dancers for various Christian recording artists. It was while they were rehearsing for a talent show that the threesome met members of one of

Christian music's premier bands—dc Talk. It was a meeting that would later result to be their big break.

"dc Talk was at the same theater where we were practicing, and we sang for them," Lisa recollects. "We ended up touring with them. Two years later [dc Talk member] Toby McKeehan opened up a record production company, and we were the first group signed to his label."

Since that record debut in 1994, it has been a swift road to success for Out of Eden, considered by many to be Christian music's first urban divas. Since storming the Christian music scene with their catchy gospel-tinged songs that include a mix of styles ranging from hip-hop and R&B to rap, the trio has not only been nominated for a Dove Award but in 1996 also won the National Music Award for Best R&B Group of the Year.

While grateful for all this success, Lisa remains wary about being corrupted by it—especially by such temptations as alcohol and drug abuse.

"Say we're at one of these benefit parties that we're always invited to. We want to go there as examples and not go there and let our guard slip because we're around certain people doing certain things," she asserts.

"There are lots of people in the world who call themselves Christians but really don't act like Christians. And we really want to be Christians and really be what God has called us to be. We don't ever want to sell out or do the wrong thing. So we really try to watch that. We try to be conscious of that all the time."

In one of their recent albums, *More Than You Know*, Lisa hints in a song she wrote, "Get It Right," that there have been occasions when she and her sisters sometimes slipped in their walk. The lyrics in the song have to do with "falling down to compromise."

"I had some friendships that could have easily pulled me down and messed up my testimony," she discloses. "And there were some other things where God showed us we weren't always living what we talked about from the stage. So, as the song says, we needed get it right and we did."

Yet another temptation that Lisa worries about is that of pride—something that can be difficult to contend with for young people whose debut album sold more than 150,000 copies.

Lisa states that she and her sisters try to thwart that temptation by devoting some of their time to a ministry that involves speaking before high school students, youth groups, and churches about the Word of Jesus. And pride is often a subject that they address.

Wherever they may be speaking or performing, however, the message is always straight up about Jesus.

"A lot of times people are more focused on our entertainment side, and they'd rather give attention and glory to us than to give glory where it belongs," she declares. "They forget who gave us this challenge and who gave us the opportunity and who opened the doors for us.

"It was the Lord. And with all this adulation it's very easy for us to get caught up in it all and think bigger of ourselves than we should. That's why we do ministry as well as entertainment. And that's why I read and reread this scripture.

"It's my way of remembering that God gave us all of this and He should be praised for it—not me and my sisters. That's also why when people ask for an autograph I write that scripture."

Lisa submits that another way in which Out of Eden keeps on spiritual track is by surrounding themselves with spiritual-minded people. "I have my husband and my mother and people who have known us for a long time before all this fame—and they keep us in check," she asserts. "Plus we really believe that God wants us to go into the world as examples."

Returning to the subject of pride, the talented performer submits that she also sometimes worries about a more subtle form of that sin. "Sometimes there's something else besides outward displays of pride," she explains. "There's more than 'Hello, I'm the greatest, look at me.'

"Sometimes there's more of a heart thing where you're

thinking: 'I shouldn't have to do that because I've sold so many records. So why do I have to do this?' You don't really voice it because you know that pride is wrong, and you don't want anybody to know that you're prideful.

"It's more in the heart. And that's just as bad as being like, you know, 'I'm the greatest. Everybody get out of my way.' So I've had to deal with this heart thing."

The attractive singer, known for her gusty melodies, credits scripture for helping her to check this tendency. "Scripture is the Word of God," she professes. "You can't find anything more powerful than that.

"In the Old Testament and in the New Testament these were the words that the prophets got direct from God. They wrote these words for us to breathe and walk by, and that's what I try to do to avoid things like pride."

As Out of Eden's main lyricist, Lisa hopes her songwriting talents make some small contribution in that direction. "The best experience for me is when the concert is over and one person comes up and says, 'I never understood the love of the Lord no matter how many times my youth pastor explained it. But from you it makes sense.'"

Nowadays, despite her busy schedule, Lisa offers that she still puts time aside each month for a reading of Romans 12 and Ephesians. "I read that just to keep me in check and make me remember how I'm supposed to be living my life.

It tells how we're supposed to be living a holy life and hate evil."

That statement brings to mind another of her favorite scriptures. "It's Isaiah 55: 7, and it reminds me of the forgiveness of the Lord if I feel I've done something wrong," she professes.

"You know, the Devil can come and make us think that we're bad—that we can never be a good Christian or whatever. But this scripture says that God is there to forgive us, and to help us be better." She goes on to quote the verse: " 'Let the wicked forsake his way and the unrighteous man his thoughts; and let him return unto the Lord, and he will have mercy upon him; and to our God, for he will abundantly pardon.' "

Lisa discloses that although she always tries to devote time to formal prayer, there are days when that is not possible. "God is my friend and I find myself driving around in my car and, instead of talking to myself, I just pray to God or carry on a conversation with Him.

"He doesn't just want us to commune with Him on our knees," she continues. "He wants us to commune with Him throughout the day. He is our Heavenly Father, and when you have a relationship with someone, you want to talk with him all the time. God is the ultimate counselor."

The peace that God has brought into her own life is available to anyone who desires it, Lisa submits. She affirms that all that is required is a reading of scripture and prayer.

"Scripture is encouragement. It's comfort. It's peace—it's all of that," she testifies. "Reading the Word will keep you out of crises and it will assist you if you are in crises. If you're constantly renewing the Word of God in your mind, and you're feeding on that, then the spirit will always be stronger than the flesh."

Lisa Daggs

I waited patiently for the Lord; and he in-clined unto me, and heard my cry.

He brought me up also out of a horrible pit, out of the miry clay, and set my feet upon a rock, and established my goings.

And he hath put a new song in my mouth, even praise unto our God: many shall see it, and fear, and shall trust in the Lord.

PSALM 40:1-3

CHRISTIAN COUNTRY MUSIC STAR Lisa Daggs holds a special candle for those in recovery programs, because the talented singer and songwriter, who in 1996 was voted New Artist of the Year by the Christian Country Music Association, nearly destroyed her own life through alcohol and drug abuse.

Frustrated by her failure in the 1980s to break into the Nashville music scene as a country gospel artist, Lisa recalls "falling away from the Lord." The Dove nominee with the crystalline voice and warm, natural rapport with her audiences spiraled into substance abuse, which continued while later performing on the fast-paced Nevada nightclub circuit.

Having spiritually and emotionally bottomed out, Lisa rededicated her life to the Lord and put her addictive lifestyle behind her. As a result, the California native attests that today she has rediscovered the inner peace that she had forgotten.

Nowadays Lisa, who is involved in a full-time ministry—the Lisa D. Ministries—never ceases to praise God for bringing her out of what she describes as a "horrible pit." Through her insightful lyrics and powerful personal testimony, she frequently shares her past ordeal with her audiences.

"I don't know how patiently I did wait for the Lord," she submits, "but I did wait for Him. And He turned to me. He got me out of the mess I was in and set my feet on a rock.

He gave me a new song and I read this scripture to remind me of that."

LISA DAGGS SPARES NO WORDS IN DESCRIBING her life as a failure until she found "the restorative grace of Jesus Christ."

In fact, the attractive blond, hazel-eyed Cheyenne Records artist is more than eager to share her courageous story with her audiences, hoping that by doing so she will help anyone feeling depressed or caught up in an addictive lifestyle to turn to the Lord for help.

Her feelings about God's grace are summed up in one of her hit singles, "You First Loved Me":

If anyone had told me
I'd be standing here today,
I would have looked at them
and laughed, then turned and walked away.
But I'll tell the world my failures, my human
circumstances,
and how You pulled me from
such ruin.
You're the God of second chances.

Although raised in a religious household, Lisa believes her rebellion against the Lord began at age ten, when her parents divorced.

"When that happened I tried to run faster than God's plan for my life," she declares. "My dad was the greatest hero in my life and I didn't really get to know him that well—but the desire was there to know him. But he walked out and there was a major void in my life that I was searching to fill."

Until that point, life was fairly normal for Lisa, the youngest of three children, who was born in Los Angeles and raised in Sacramento. Lisa's father owned a chain of restaurants, while her mother was a homebody who was kept busy raising Lisa and her brothers.

Although Lisa recalls that religion was of more importance to her mother than her father, that didn't keep her and her siblings from attending church regularly. "I was raised in the Assemblies of God church, but my mom was the only influence in Christianity that we had. My father didn't really live the life.

"We were pretty active in church. I was there with my mother every Sunday night, every Wednesday night, and nights in between when there was something going on."

It was after her parents' divorce that Lisa admits that she

began to "backslide. There was a lack in my life. As a result of not having a father, I struggled a lot with acceptance and approval and all that."

Plagued by feelings of insecurity, Lisa remembers that she began experimenting with alcohol and drugs in high school—a practice that continued through her college years.

In the meantime, the young woman who had developed a passion for music as a youngster dreamed of pursuing a career as a country gospel singer. "My dad sang in church, my mother sang, my brothers sang. I sang my first solo when I was three."

That interest led Lisa to enroll at American River College in Sacramento, where she majored in music and minored in voice. "And then I started making money singing in clubs, and I said, 'What do I need college for?' So I quit."

Soon Nashville beckoned. While in her early twenties Lisa moved to Music City to try her skills as a country gospel artist. To support herself, she worked as a studio vocalist and performed at showcases for local Nashville songwriters.

"I thought I'd come to Nashville and sing country gospel, but I ended up staying for five years and continuing the lifestyle I had started back in Sacramento. Alcohol and drugs got hold of my life in Nashville, and I lost focus of my direction."

Disillusioned about the course of her career, Lisa recollects deciding in the late 1980s to leave the Nashville scene and experience new audiences on the West Coast. There she began performing on the Nevada circuit, playing mostly country-style music at casinos throughout the state.

"I ended up singing with an all-female band and found myself in a real desperate situation," Lisa recalls. "I continued to hit the drugs and the alcohol. It had become a major part of my life—even more so in that fast-paced lifestyle on the West Coast. And I got into trouble with the law."

Lisa declines to go into the specifics of that situation but will speak about her feelings immediately afterward. "I felt like I had reached my bottom in life, both spiritually and emotionally," she submits. "I was just so disappointed with myself at this point.

"I had a tour lined up to go overseas with my band and I had to find a lead singer to take my place to go because I had gotten into trouble with the law. They went and I stayed and went into rehab."

In recalling that period of her life, Lisa offers that as bad as it was, it also served a positive purpose. "I think that's when the light was really turned on. I thought I had blown it so bad that I would never sing again and that there was no hope for any fun in my life."

The Christian country music star remembers spending much of her time in rehab reflecting upon the direction of her life.

"I realized that everything I had set out to do had kind of gone backward. I wasn't getting ahead in life and I was miserable. There wasn't peace or joy in my life or contentment. There was a continual struggle just to fill that void that I was feeling since I was a young child.

"It was time to look inside myself and find what was missing. And for me it was a relationship with God. So on November 11, 1989, I went into a twelve-step treatment program and I received the tools that I needed to learn how to deal with life in a more healthy fashion."

For Lisa, however, the real turning point came when she accepted Christ into her life.

"There were so many times before this when I found things weren't going right I would run back to church to try and make it right. Then I would go back to drinking or doing drugs. This was before I had known all about Christ. But this time I was real serious about it. This time I was ready not just to bargain with God but to keep my side of the bargain.

"And so about two months after I got clean and sober I finally surrendered my life and my heart to God—and look what he's done for me! No way seven and a half years ago did I ever think that I'd be going around singing Christian music and telling people of my failures and hope that they would find faith in their lives and not be discouraged or downtrodden—telling them that if He could do this for me, look what He could do for you. All you have to do is receive Him."

Lisa remembers it was on a cold, winter day in January 1990 when she experienced her religious conversion. She was in a women's rehab program at the time in Carmichael, California, and her mother had just made arrangements to get her out on a pass.

"It was pretty amazing that my mom—who I feel is like my personal angel and who prayed steadily for me before I was a Christian—was able to get me a pass to go out," Lisa declares.

"Then she told me we were going to visit a friend and her daughter who she had been praying with. The woman's daughter had also had a rough bout with life, but now she was straight. And I thought my mom and I were just going to go over and reminisce with those two people and say how wonderful it was that we were clean and that we weren't using or drinking."

But in the hours to come, Lisa would experience more than just polite conversation. Today Lisa reflects upon that meeting as "part of God's ultimate plan for me.

"They had a prayer cove in their house—they were wealthy people," she recalls. "As we started walking down this rock pit that was built for prayer and devotion, I suddenly felt like something was going to have to give. I could feel it in my spirit."

Lisa still remembers feeling a bit disturbed by this feeling and struggling against it. "I didn't know if I was really ready for this. I was ready to give God that day all the fear that I had for my future, because I was in trouble.

"But I wasn't sure whether I was ready to give Him all the secret desires of my heart. I was full of self-will—running my own show, believing that I knew what was best for my life."

Lisa recalls feeling startled when, just as she was thinking those words, the woman's daughter turned to her and said: "You know, you're going to have to give it up. You're going to have to let Him do what He wants in your life if you're ever to sing again.

"In that moment I became willing to turn my life over to the complete care of God, trusting in Him for strength and guidance. It wasn't easy, but I did it. I remember being completely broken that day. And I completely rededicated my life to Him and my life has changed dramatically. I released everything to the Lord—including my dreams.

"Whatever His plan was it would have to be better than what I had done with my life. It was the ultimate step of faith, and it's been a continual path each day closer to Him."

Nowadays the recently married entertainer Lisa lives in Nashville with her husband and a renewed sense of peace in her life. Lisa asserts that she has not forgotten the long, rocky road that she's traveled, often reading her favorite scripture in order to remind her of God's grace. "There's power in scripture. I think we find our strength here. Faith comes by hearing and hearing comes by the Word."

When performing onstage, Lisa often focuses on her own restoration. Through songs and testimony, she tells audiences that it isn't sufficient simply to be clean and sober but that they must "also embrace Christ in their heart. If you don't have Him in your heart, there's still a void."

Although life these days seems to be going well for the Christian artist, she confesses to moments when she feels a bit down. Lisa says it is during such moments that she quickly turns to her favorite scripture.

"This scripture helps to build faith especially if you're in a blue mood or feeling a little discouraged," she counsels. "It lifts me up. It helps me feel more connected with the Lord."

For anyone suffering from substance abuse, Lisa offers

these words of advice, as someone who has been there: "Just set it down. Lay it down and don't pick it up. And just try to take it one minute at a time.

"There are a lot of recovery programs out there that you can get involved in. If you're sick and tired of being sick and tired, just lay it down and reach out to places where you can get help.

"And pray. Step into faith and ask God to help you through it and He will. And read this scripture. It will help. It takes some bravery—some courage—to find out who you are and not do it under the influence of a bottle. But I'm proof that you can start over again."

Margaret Becker

Trust in the Lord, and do good; so *shalt thou dwell in the land, and verily thou shalt be fed.*
Delight thyself also in the Lord; and he shall give thee the desires of thine heart.

PSALM 37:3 — 4

UNTIL SHE LEARNED TO TRUST IN the Lord rather than trying to dictate how her life should be led, two-time Dove winner and three-time Grammy nominee Margaret Becker wasn't even certain she should pursue a career in Christian music.

The singer and songwriter further worried that her musical ambition had become an "idol" more important to her than the worship of the Lord. So, instead of utilizing her God-given talents, the New York native worked odd jobs that often left her feeling frustrated and unfulfilled.

It was a reading of Psalm 37 that helped to convince Margaret that a career in music was right for her. "That scripture became my light in the darkness," she proclaims. "There are certain points in your life where God alone can bring growth and change, and you just have to wait for His timing.

"After reading that scripture I just stepped back from it all and asked Him to place the correct desires in my heart. I stopped asking him for what I thought I needed, and I stopped trying to control things."

Today the thirty-seven-year-old Christian music superstar is not only on the right path, but she also shares with others what she has found through songs that reflect hope, faith, and, above all, a trust in the Lord.

———

IT'S EASY TO LOOK AT ANY OF MARGARET
Becker's album covers and assume that the attractive woman
with the reddish hair, freckles, and smiling eyes gazing back
at you is the portrait of a woman who has led a carefree life.

But when Margaret shares her testimony, what emerges
instead is a portrait of a deeply sensitive and introspective
human being who continues to wrestle with such issues as
God's forgiveness, love, and mercy.

It's her sensitive quality that leaves her most vulnerable,
she confides. "That's the most difficult thing about me. I'm
a very, very, very sensitive person emotionally, and my sen-
sitivity makes me an easy target.

"Sure, it's great to have a career that I've always wanted,
but the nature of my vocation dictates that I have to bare
my soul in a public arena—and that opens a floodgate of
responses, not all of them godly."

The youngest of four children born in Long Island to a
first-generation, hardworking German father and an Irish
mother, Margaret recalls that religion and music both played
an important part in her upbringing.

"My mother was a very devout Catholic and my father
was Episcopalian. Both of them were very focused on Christ
and focused on the fact that God is the ultimate authority
and that He is also the ultimate saver."

Music also absorbed her at an early age. Margaret remembers always fantasizing about becoming a singer, and, while still in high school, she performed at various Greenwich Village jazz clubs.

As the years progressed, Margaret developed another interest—to grow in her relationship with God. "I always had a good knowledge of the Lord, but I wanted more from my faith," she offers. "I wanted to have a richer experience as a Christian."

That desire began to conflict with her dream of a career as a performer. "I worried that my ambition had become an idol," she recollects. "So for more than two years I didn't pick up a guitar or sing a song. I told God, 'I don't need to do this.'

"It was a time when I wasn't really sure what I was going to be doing the rest of my life. I knew what I wanted to do—I wanted to write music and I wanted to sing—but I wasn't sure that was God's will."

There was also the reality that as a songwriter, her career wasn't really going anywhere. Living in New York City was an expensive proposition, and Margaret, always the practical type, decided to seek jobs that offered benefits. "It seemed that every door that led to the fulfillment of my goal as a performer was closing on me. So I decided to put aside music for a while."

Margaret eventually took a job as a bill collector for Sears and supplemented her income by giving private music lessons. "There was a period when I was working four jobs and I did that for four years," she recalls. "Sometimes I would go for months without a day off. It was a very stressful time of life for me."

Although she had gained some financial security, Margaret remembers sensing that "there was something wrong here. I was thoroughly confused and frustrated," she recalls, "but I still kept trying to walk away from my music and writing. And I was doing a lot of fasting and praying during that time."

It was shortly after her twenty-third birthday that Margaret rediscovered a scripture that would dramatically alter her life. "I came across Psalm 37 and my eyes were open to it in a different way than all the other times that I had read it—especially verse four where it says 'Delight thyself also in the Lord; and he shall give thee the desires of thine heart.'

"When I read it at this particular time—in the midst of my struggles—it took on a different shading. I read it as '*He* will place the correct desire in your heart. And perhaps it will be a surprise to you—but that desire will be the correct one for you.' "

Margaret remembers the impact those words had on her.

"It wasn't like there was an immediate change in my life. It's not like everything suddenly became good," she recollects. "But it was a turning point in my struggle when I stopped asking Him for what *I* thought *I* needed and wiped the slate clean as much as is humanly possible. I asked Him to place the correct desires in my heart. I turned my life over to Him and his purposes."

In hindsight, Margaret today recognizes that it probably always was God's intention to have her perform music as a way to minister to people—but that she was too busy trying to dictate her life to do so.

Now that she decided to see what God wanted her to do, things began to change.

First a friend encouraged Margaret to pick up her guitar, which she did—performing at youth groups and missions throughout New York. Margaret can still remember how good it felt to have that guitar in her hands again. "I thought, if this is one way You can use me, Lord, great."

Still, she remembers how she resisted pursuing her career any further. Then another friend entered the picture, admonishing Margaret for "spinning her wheels."

Margaret recalls heeding her friend's advice when he advised her to go to Nashville to see what came of it. "I managed to save enough money to live there for a while.

And then I began to make the rounds of record companies. I said, 'Here I am, are you interested?' " she recalls with a chuckle.

To her surprise, several record producers were. "I had a contract within three weeks. Doors were suddenly opening for me, and I thought, 'Well, I guess this is what I was supposed to do.' That's when I started to take my music seriously."

Margaret continues to be grateful for the psalm that helped to change the course of her life. "That verse came to me at one of the most difficult times in my life. And it keeps coming back to me as an absolute truth. It's always my light in the darkness, and it's part of my thought structure—my very being."

If Margaret has any regrets, it's that she didn't learn to trust in the Lord sooner rather than later. "If you're afraid to do what feels right for you—if you always stay with what's safe—then in a way you're trying to control the situation. You're dictating what God can do with you."

For those similarly gripped by fear or uncertainty, Margaret advises them to focus on her favorite scripture as well as the rest of God's words. "Scriptures are the ultimate healing words, the ultimate substance that a soul can ever acquire," she enthuses. "You can always find scriptures that either directly or indirectly deal with your struggle.

"Memorize them. Commit them to your entire being because you need to fight your interior battle before you fight your exterior battle. You should choose the weapons that God has provided, and those would be His words that are found in scripture."

Neal Coomer

These things I have spoken unto you, that in me ye might have peace. In the world ye shall have tribulation: but be of good cheer; I have overcome the world.

JOHN 16:33

NEAL COOMER, FORMERLY OF THE duo East to West, believes that he has twice successfully engaged in spiritual warfare against the Devil in a battle for his soul.

The twenty-eight-year-old Dove-nominated artist, who, until May 1, 1997, shared singing duties with partner Jay DeMarcus in one of the most popular duos on the contemporary Christian music scene, attributes his victories to a firm faith in the greater power of the Lord, a reading of scripture, and prayer.

The ordinarily upbeat Louisville, Kentucky, native and son of a Church-of-God evangelist recalls that on both occasions he inexplicably found himself gripped by depression so severe that at one point he even considered taking his own life.

Today Neal is convinced that both attacks were orchestrated by Satan, who wanted to thwart his musical ministry with East to West. He further believes that without a reading of scripture—particularly the verses from John, Corinthians, and the Psalms—Satan might have achieved his goal.

"When Jesus was battling against Satan, what did He do? He always pulled scripture," Neal proclaims. "The scriptures tell us 'you shall know the truth and the truth shall make you free.' "

NEAL COOMER HAS HAD HIS FAIR SHARE OF life's setbacks, including the agony of his parents' divorce when he was only eleven, and the loss of his two beloved grandparents.

But none of those travails comes close to the mental agony he suffered on two separate occasions—the first when he was a nineteen-year-old college student—as a result of mysterious bouts of depression.

The handsome singer with the boy-next-door looks and voice that imparts friendliness and warmth to all who listen still thanks the Lord for scripture, which Neal attests got him through those psychologically disabling episodes.

"Those were the times when scripture became so meaningful and alive to me—even more so than in my everyday life," Neal recollects. "They really spoke to me."

Neal further credits his religious upbringing for helping him survive his struggles with Satan. "I was raised in the church and I always had a good relationship and a walk with God," he submits. "I've always had a heart of God.

"But it was when I was in college that I really made the effort of transferring that knowledge from my head to my heart. That's why I went to a Christian college. I wanted to make an effort to pursue a relationship with Christ. I just wasn't all that concerned about living a Christian life until college, which is when I started looking for the Lord."

The timing of Neal's newfound relationship with God couldn't have been a better one, for in the days to come the young college student would have to rely heavily on his faith in Jesus.

Neal recalls that the first Satanic attack took place when he was a nineteen year old attending Lee College in Cleveland, Tennessee, where he was majoring in communications.

"I was in my college choir—because I grew up singing—and we were traveling. Both Jay and I grew up loving to sing, although Jay knew since he was five that he wanted to be a musician—I didn't know that back then.

"Anyway, I remember that we were in Atlanta and on our way to California. I was staying in a friend's home and one morning about six-thirty—and this was the first and only time that this ever happened to me—I suddenly woke up and felt like there was a real evil presence around me.

"It might sound corny to some people, but I felt a real serious oppression. I woke my friend up because it was so disturbing—I mean, it was to the point where I felt I was going to need some help or something. I wasn't a depressed person before, and I'm not a depressed person now, so I didn't understand what was happening to me."

Neal can't recall any physical phenomenon, but what he does remember is that "I really felt that there was a spiritual battle going on for my soul. It still feels a little spooky to even say it. It got to a point where there were thoughts in my head about suicide—which is the first time that ever happened to me."

As the assault continued, the Christian music star remembers sinking deeper and deeper into gloomy, self-destructive thoughts.

"I felt like I wasn't going to rise above this, so I should stop making myself miserable—that I should end my life and get it over with. I woke my friend up and I was crying and telling him that I didn't know what was going on. I was pretty disturbed and telling him about what I was thinking. I said, 'This is what's ringing in my head and I don't know what to do.' "

But Neal's friend immediately knew what to do.

"He gave me a scripture that I still have written down on the piece of paper that he gave it to me on—and that's been almost ten years ago," Neal relates. He begins to quote, from Corinthians II: " '*We are* troubled on every side, yet not distressed; *we are* perplexed, but not in despair; persecuted, but not forsaken; cast down, but not destroyed.' "

Neal can recall reading and rereading that verse through most of the day until, to his delight, his feelings of depression slowly began to lift. "This verse was awesome when I was feeling afflicted," he proclaims.

"I mean, where do we go when we have a hard time and

we have troubles and struggles? We find out we're not as independent as we think we are and we express our dependence on God. And I think it's in those times of crises that God and the scriptures becomes so real to us as they did to me during those moments."

His spiritual recovery received an unexpected boost two days later when a mysterious stranger approached him after a choir performance in a California church.

"This stranger he just walked up to me and he said, 'Look, I don't know you from anyone. I just feel like the Lord is telling me to tell you this.' And he quoted Luke 10:19 to me. The words in that scripture are about overcoming the enemy and nothing will harm you, and they really spoke to me. He was dead on about what was going on in my life at the time.

"And he went on to encourage me and speak to me. Although my confidence was improving over the past couple of days, that night my confidence greatly improved. I was realizing that you don't have to live defeated or discouraged. I stood on those words. I was really on the mountain after that."

Things returned to normal for Neal, who thought he had seen the last of spiritual warfare with Satan. He was wrong. Six years later, at age twenty-five, Neal again found himself engulfed by those same unexplained feelings of depression.

"I was again going through some serious depression. It

was a cycle that lasted for a while, and, again, I went back to the scriptures. That's when the Psalms with their messages of hope became spirit to me. It was also when I started reading the scripture from John.

"I learned that scripture by heart and read it over and over again. It was John, the Psalms, and a book I was reading at the time—*The Bondage Breaker*—that helped me get through this second attack."

Today the Benson Records star has enjoyed a career with a pop music duo that stormed the Christian music world and picked up a pair of Best New Artist nominations along the way. And he is grateful not only for those honors but that East to West could spread God's message in the process.

"Jay and I were in the beginning stages of making this happen back then and I think it was an effort by Satan to stop what we were embarking on," he offers.

"There was a time when I thought that the idea of spiritual warfare was a bit too charismatic for me," he continues, "but it's not. You can be a conservative Episcopalian and still might have to deal with spiritual warfare."

His warfare with Satan has convinced Neal that it is not necessary to feel stronger than the Devil in order to defeat him but simply to entertain the knowledge that Satan is capable of lies and deceptions.

"What the Word says is that 'we shall know the truth and the truth shall make us free.' It doesn't say by your power and authority will you be free. The word just talks about knowing the truth.

"When Jesus was battling against Satan, what did he do? He always pulled scripture. It's all about exposing the lies. Satan always tries to deceive us, and we're truly deceived when we no longer believe the truth. It's a truth issue, not a power issue."

Neal counsels anyone suffering from depression to first try to determine whether there are demonic forces at work. "I believe when there's depression a lot of times there can be a spiritual issue and we just don't realize it," he submits.

"I also believe that you should also seek out a godly person—whether it be a counselor, a therapist, or a church staff member—because there are a lot of psychological and emotional issues involved that need to be dealt with."

Above all, Neal counsels faith and a reading of scripture. "As an artist and in my personal life, I just want to let people know that no matter how frail we are as humans, we know our strength lies with Jesus Christ."

Eddie Carswell

*That I may know him, and the power of his
resurrection, and the fellowship of his sufferings,
being made conformable unto his death . . .*

PHILIPPIANS 3:10

EDDIE CARSWELL, NEWSONG'S FOUND-ing member, believes he was lost to God before being saved at age twenty-six. As a result, he advocates an annual spiritual checkup for Christians because he believes many of them are unknowingly in the same predicament.

"The first question on the list should be whether you've ever asked Jesus Christ into your life," asserts the forty-seven-year-old Georgian native, who shares vocal duties with fellow founder Billy Goodwin and lead singer Russ Lee.

He also suggests a reading of his favorite scripture from Philippians.

"This scripture is important," Eddie declares. "Reading it is another part of your checkup. You may think you know Him, but this will remind you to know Him more and to pursue Him and press toward the right mark. It's a verse of encouragement telling us not to grow weary or lose sight of why you're here."

WHEN A BAND RECORDS A NUMBER-ONE HIT song that remains on the top of the Christian radio charts for three consecutive weeks, you might expect it to be a cause for celebration for its leader.

But while Eddie Carswell admits he is truly delighted by the news, he is also working hard to keep his emotions in check, asserting that he wants to reserve his enthusiasm for what really matters in his life—Jesus.

"Sure, I'm real excited that we got the number-one song in the United States the third week in the row this week on Christian radio," declares the tall, blond, and blue-eyed performer in a voice thickly laced with a Georgia drawl.

"But if I don't watch out I'll get more worried about 'Okay, can we get another number one on the next song?' and 'How many albums are going to sell?' I don't want to get caught up in all that.

"It's important what we've accomplished, but it's not as important as knowing Him, the power of His resurrection, and the fellowship of His suffering. It's the pressing toward the mark of God Christ Jesus that is more important, and the scripture from Philippians is a reminder to me that I need to press toward the mark—not the money."

It's a lesson that Eddie and the other four members who comprise this top-of-the-charts contemporary pop band seem not to have lost track of since NewSong was founded in 1981 as a vocal quartet.

Although today there's a new band format and a whole new look to the group—not to mention the many accolades NewSong has chalked up since its founding—what has remained consistent is the five men's devotion to ministry.

"What we're trying to say to people is that there's nothing

better than Jesus," offers vocalist Russ Lee. It's a sentiment that Eddie shares. "All of our affections and lives and faith are pointed to who He is and being with Him," he proclaims.

That message is one that members of NewSong, winners of a Dove nomination in 1994 for Group of the Year and, another, in 1996, for Contemporary Album of the Year, try to demonstrate both on and off the stage.

"That's why the verse from Philippians is a good verse even for people who know Him to study," Eddie proclaims of his favorite scripture. "You may know Him, but this will help you want to know Him even more and make you not lose sight of why you're here.

"You've got to pursue the right things. We live in a real business, high-pressure, go-get-'em world, and this scripture will help you make sure you're doing things for the right reasons."

It's a lesson that the talented singer and songwriter sadly admits he failed to grasp until his marriage in 1976.

Although he recalls growing up in a religious household in Tifton, Georgia, where he was the youngest of four siblings—one brother and two sisters—Eddie can remember attending lots of church services but not feeling any real emotional ties to the Lord back then.

"I was raised in a family that always went to church," he reminisces. "My mother was a beautician, and my father was a supervisor in a factory, and they took us to the Primitive Baptist Church. Actually, it was considered somewhat progressive because it had a piano there," he chuckles.

"Later on, when we were all grown, we started going to a real fundamental church where there was no keyboard—people just sang. So although I've always believed in the Lord, and although twenty-six years of my life involves being around church, I actually didn't come to know Him until I was twenty-six years old and got saved. Yeah, I went to church a lot, but it never got past my ears to my heart."

Eddie concedes he might have remained lost had he not tied the knot in 1976 with Terrie, his current wife of twenty-one years, a young woman he first met while in high school.

"That's when I came to know the Lord and got saved," he professes. "Terrie witnessed to me about the need to get baptized. She thought that was what was wrong with me and what was wrong about our marriage—that I needed that.

"So I went and had lunch with her pastor, and he asked me if I was a Christian. I said, 'Yes, I might be. If you'd explain to me what one is, I can tell you if I am. I'm not sure.'

"Once he explained it all to me, I realized I wasn't—that I really wasn't practicing my Christianity. I learned that being Christian means that you ask Jesus into your heart, you have your life changed, and old things become new."

Eddie pauses, continuing with a chuckle. "After a bunch of talking that day I got saved on my lunch hour. I went back to Terrie and said, 'Some of the stuff he told me was not what you were telling me.'

"That Sunday morning the pastor asked us both to come in and talk to him. He asked Terrie if she knew if she was a Christian. Terri went home that afternoon and asked Jesus to come into her heart. That evening we both got baptized."

Eddie remembers how his new relationship with God deepened while attending a Bible conference in Dallas, Texas. "That was about ten years ago—it's when NewSong first started and we were doing more church-related events. I was doing this Bible conference and this one preacher preached this scripture from Philippians.

"There was more to it—the whole message—but I just kind of grabbed on to this verse. It challenged me to know Him and the power of His resurrection. It really spoke to my heart. That kind of became my goal in life, and I even wrote a song around this verse. I still haven't attained that goal—I'm not true to it every second of my life—but I'm heading that way."

Turning to his passion for music, Eddie recalls that writing always has interested him. "I remember as far back as kindergarten and first grade I would write down the lyrics of songs and give them to girls or show them to my parents or whatever.

"I was always writing a song or doing something. And my mother was encouraging about it, although she once told me it wouldn't amount to much unless I wrote music that praised the Lord."

In high school, writing was a way for the Georgia teenager to overcome his shyness. "I was pretty much a timid person compared to what I am now," he recollects. "But through my writing my teachers used to encourage me. It was like a light went on—'Hey, all right, this is something that I do well.' I think the Lord was just using my mother to encourage me in that direction."

Eddie went on to Georgia's Valdosta State University, where he majored in management. While in school, he worked part time writing jingles for regional radio commercials. It was a period of his life when the Christian music star's spiritual life was on the back burner.

"There was no church for me except for an occasional Easter Sunday or something like that. For twenty-six years I was raised in a family that had gone to church, but now I was lost."

Today that is no longer true. The immensely talented performer is a committed Christian, and he is dedicated to helping others find the Lord, as well. Much of the way Eddie gets that message across is through his musical ministry with NewSong.

Which, again, brings him back to the subject of his favorite scripture, one that he says is never far from his mind. "Doing what I do—this ministry around the country and using Christian music to do it as a vehicle—I'm asked a lot about what my favorite verse is.

"So I have quite a lot of opportunities to write it down on somebody's Bible or on a poster. It helps people who have been Christians a long time to think about their relationship with the Lord in a new, refreshing way.

"Doing that helps me, as well. It reminds me again to stay on target—to know Him better and share that with those I come in contact with. I need to be reminded, too. I think we're all struggling in some area, in some way with something, and trying to be closer to the Lord is going to help us through these hard times."

NewSong's leader also advocates an annual spiritual checkup, which he believes will help determine whether a person is lost or saved.

"A good checkup would be to ask yourself if you ever asked Jesus Christ to come into your heart. Or do you think you should go to heaven just because you feel that you're a good person?

"If you feel a lack of peace or emptiness—and you can't

exactly identify what the problem is—maybe you're feeling that because of being lost and it's something only Jesus can fill.

"It's like the Bible says. I don't know the exact words, but it's something about making sure you're in the faith. So I think it's definitely worth the time to give yourself a spiritual checkup and see where you are."

These are questions that Eddie says he often asks himself, before meditating on his favorite scripture.

"For me scripture is the light to the path," he proclaims. "It's encouraging, it's soothing, and it gives me the vision to do things. I always find myself in a place—whether it's on the business side with the band or in my personal life—where I need to lean on the Lord and to press in on Him to find out where I'm going.

"I don't know what I'd do without scripture or prayer. I think we're all struggling in some area in some way and with something. That's why I enjoy this verse."

Randy Phillips

For I know the thoughts that I think toward you, saith the Lord, thoughts of peace, and not of evil, to give you an expected end.

Then shall ye call upon me, and ye shall go and pray unto me, and I will harken unto you.

Then shall ye seek me, and find me, when ye shall search for me with all your heart.

JEREMIAH 29:11–13

SINGER AND SONGWRITER RANDY Phillips can remember a time when he was drowning in a sea of depression and how a reading of Jeremiah helped to keep him afloat.

Randy, part of Phillips, Craig & Dean, a wildly popular contemporary Christian trio with a smooth pop sound that has received several Dove nominations, declines to go into detail about his malady, but he is quite vocal in asserting that Satan was behind its onset.

As a result, the thirty-five-year-old son of an Alexandria, Louisiana, preacherman, who has a duel career as a full-time pastor at his father's Texas church, encourages anyone wracked by depression to read scripture, trust in Christ, and seek out fellow church members for support.

"Reading the Word of God will give you hope for sure," he asserts, "but standing with someone who has been through this situation will keep you from breaking."

RANDY PHILLIPS IS FOND OF QUOTING THE PASsage from Jeremiah where the Old Testament prophet urges the Israelites not to abandon faith in God despite the severe persecution and pressure they are experiencing.

"They were suffering great disillusionment and were really down," Randy emphasizes in a Southern tenor drawl, relating it to a time in his own life when he felt similarly.

"Right there the Lord tells the Israelites through Jeremiah that He has plans for them and they're plans for good—not for evil.

"That's easy to say when everything's going well—you got money in the bank, your kids are healthy, and your career is going well—but this was really a dark season in the Israelites' life when the prophet spoke these words. Jeremiah tells them that the Lord has a plan for them—and it's for good and not for evil, and that He will bring them a future and a hope."

The singing preacher, who when he is not performing to sellout concert audiences with partners Shawn and Dan can be found tending to his flock at the World of Pentecost Church in Austin, Texas, where his parents are senior co-pastors, asserts that this passage is an excellent source of inspiration.

"I just love that scripture," Randy professes. "I've quoted it many times to people in my church who are facing loved ones who are dying, or have careers that have fallen on hard times, or people whose children have gone astray. I tell them to believe that despite their various hardships the Lord has a positive plan for them.

"We don't always understand everything, but we know He has a plan. I tell my parishioners that if they will follow

Him, it will be a good plan—and not an evil one. And these words have given people a tremendous amount of hope."

Randy recalls one instance where a woman whose father suffered a massive heart attack was cheered by this scripture.

"She was so distraught when I went to the hospital and visited her in the intensive care unit, but I was able to bring her that scripture and it just brought her fresh hope," he asserts. "It gave her the Word of the Lord to hold on to. It was a lamp unto her feet."

Hopelessness and despair are not things that this Louisiana son of a preacherman is a stranger to. And Randy credits a reading of Jeremiah for helping to get him through those dark moments.

"I don't really want to elaborate on what happened to me—it's too close and too personal," he declares. "But there was a time and point in my life when I suffered severe depression. I was absolutely at the end of myself.

"I was reading the Bible and I happened across that scripture. It just blew open my spirit. It's come to mean so much to me, and I've been able to share that with others who have undergone similar situations. It gives you faith that God has a plan."

Randy has little doubt that he was guided by the Lord to locate that verse. "It's not a scripture that is commonly read," he submits. "You know, if you're going to read the Bible, you don't ordinarily read Jeremiah because it's too depressing. I don't even remember how I got to it, but I was able to come across it."

Randy believes that his illness was initiated by Satan at a time when the smooth-voiced trio—comprised of three ministers' sons—were on the verge of success with their musical ministry. "He would have liked to destroy our ministry with its message to trust in Christ," he declares.

Randy affirms that, in his pastoral duties, he has witnessed other cases of depression that he believes were initiated by Satan. "It's one of the many tools that he can use," Randy attests. "What he would love to do is isolate you, put you off, and let you think only about your situation—how bad it is and how it's not going to get any better.

"That's the whole route of suicide—to make you feel that it can't get any better. The Bible says that the enemy has come to 'kill, still, and destroy.' That's the only thing the Devil does, and one of his methods is depression."

Randy further recommends that anyone suffering from depression should seek out the support and encouragement of other spiritually minded people besides praying and reading scripture.

"Reading the Word of God give you hope for sure," he professes, "but getting together with someone who has come through similar circumstances is absolutely incredible because it is the word of our testimony that brings faith to another person.

"No one has ever undergone something by themselves. There's always someone somewhere who has undergone the same situation. If you can get with that person and say, 'How did you make it through?' I'm telling you, it will bring you back to life.

"The Bible says a 'threefold chord is not easily broken.' There's something about standing with someone. If two or three people stand with someone, that person is not going to break. They're going to get stronger.

"That helped me make it through—the prayers of great people around me, being connected to my church, and attending services that were power packed and where the spirit of the Lord brought me up. And then there was my reading of the Word, which was the light unto my feet."

Randy, who states that he has not has not experienced any recurrence of depression since the time of his spiritual warfare against Satan, cautions that for scripture to be effective, people must believe that those words are God inspired with every fiber of their hearts.

"They're just words until you apply them—and that requires faith," proclaims the Buddy Holly lookalike, who today lives with his wife, Denise, and daughter, Garland, in

Austin, Texas. "It's the faith in reading the Word that is the breath of God. Otherwise it's just dead print.

"When you have faith, when you reach out and grab it and apply it to your life, it suddenly becomes personal words that brings life to any situation. When you seize these words of God with faith and say 'This is for me,' they come alive and they can revive you."

That type of faith is something that Randy can recollect being familiar with for most of his life. The parents of Randy and his younger sister were both evangelist preachers.

Randy still remembers as a young boy traveling with his parents and sister to revival meetings throughout Louisiana from his birthplace of Alexandria.

"We'd go from church to church and I'd sing at these great revivals," he recalls. "My dad was a great evangelist for the Pentecostal movement in the 1950s, and I'd find myself as an eight-year-old singing in front of 10,000 people at a camp meeting. Church and music is really all I've ever known. I've never known any other life, really."

But Randy adds not until his twelfth birthday did faith take on an extra-special meaning to him. "I had an encounter with God that was so incredible, that He lived in me," he enthusiastically declares. "For the very first time I lived what I was singing and I experienced what I was saying."

That event took place one evening in a church whose

name Randy can no longer recall. "I walked toward the front of the church to get the crown of the Lord. I was just twelve, but I repented of all the things I had done wrong."

He chuckles at the memory. "I know twelve is a little young to be repenting things, but there were some things I needed to get right. That night the Lord came into my life. I was filled with the Holy Spirit. I spoke with tongues, and it changed me and empowered me. When I walked out of that church I was simply transformed."

Today Randy and his two partners, also full-time pastors at their local churches, try to share that special feeling with their concert audiences as well as their congregations. "What we do in concert is just an extension of our local ministries," he declares.

"We have definitely been blessed to be able to serve the Lord as full-time pastors and also as musicians, and we love both sides of our ministries. Our music speaks to people's hearts, and our roles as pastors keep us in touch with real people with real problems."

Rebecca St. James

But none of these things move me, neither count I my life dear unto myself, so that I might finish my course with joy, and the ministry, which I have received of the Lord Jesus, to testify the gospel of the grace of God.

ACTS 20:24

AUSTRALIAN SINGING SENSATION Rebecca St. James, who has been described as "part Amy Grant, part Mother Teresa, and part Billy Graham," was once so destitute that she and her family found themselves cleaning houses, mowing lawns, baby-sitting, and doing other odd jobs in order to survive financially.

But miracles can happen, and the beautiful twenty-year-old Grammy and two-time Dove nominee affirms that she experienced several of them that helped bring her and her family through their ordeal—topped off by a recording contract at age sixteen.

The brown-haired and brown-eyed Aussie transplant, who in 1997 was voted Favorite Female Vocalist by readers of *CCM* and *Campus Life* magazines, credits faith, prayer, and a reading of scripture for her family's reversal of fortune.

Today the young Forefront Records star is busy trying to repay the Lord for His kindness through her musical ministry, as well as by her offstage devotion to sharing God's gospel—such as her recently completed book of journal entries and devotions.

Rebecca credits the verse from Acts for inspiring her in much of her evangelical work.

"It's a verse that challenges us as well as shapes our lives," she proclaims. "It remind us that even when we're in the midst of something and it looks just awful, God's words can bring us through the fire—to make us more like Him."

EVEN BEFORE THE INTERVIEW BEGINS, REBECCA St. James establishes her priorities. She requests that there be a silent moment of prayer.

For anyone who personally knows the talented young singer and songwriter, or listens to her inspired and exuberant pop tunes filled with tribute to the Lord, there is little doubt that this woman is on a mission from God—and that mission is to spread His Word.

"The most important thing for me is to complete my mission—the work Jesus the Lord gave me to tell people the good news about God's grace," Rebecca attests in an Australian-accented voice. "That's what my whole life is about—it's about God."

Rebecca submits that she selected the verse from Acts as her favorite scripture because it serves to remind her that God is more important than any personal considerations. "It's a call to us not to focus on ourselves and to focus on what we're called to do—our mission in life," she declares. "It's about giving our all to God and to love Him and serve Him—it's a focus verse."

Serving God is a lesson that Rebecca learned early in life

while growing up. "Our parents were strong believers in Christ," she asserts. "My five younger brothers and my sister and I would pray every night with them, and when my grandparents were in town we would pray with them right before we'd go to bed. I have such great memories of my family being such good models for Christ."

The talented performer says she continues to cherish those memories. "I'm so blessed to have that heritage," she enthuses. "There aren't that many Christians in Australia. My parents, my grandparents—even my great-grandmother, who's still alive at age ninety-six—are really trying to live out their faith as God would have them to do. All my brothers and sister also read the Bible and seek Him."

Rebecca remembers deciding at age thirteen, while attending a Christian school in Australia, that she wanted to serve the Lord through her gift for music. "It was 1990—that's when God started putting into my brain that maybe He wanted me to sing Christian music professionally," she recollects.

"I had grown up around Christian music all my life, because my father was involved in that whole music scene, and it was a natural and normal part of our lives. So it wasn't like a lightning bolt kind of experience. It was a sense of peace that came over me and a sense that this was where He was leading me."

Heeding that inner voice, Rebecca joined a local Christian rock band that was using music as a ministry to reach troubled young people. But that came to an end when her father's concert promotion business folded and the family decided to relocate to the United States.

Rebecca remembers settling in Nashville, where a job awaited her father. When that job also fell through, her family again found itself in dire financial straits.

"We didn't have anything," she recalls. "We didn't have any friends, we didn't have money—we didn't even have a car. What we had was each other, prayer, and the Lord."

Although the family was struggling to make ends meet, Rebecca's father decided to devote his time promoting her singing career. Soon sixteen-year-old Rebecca found herself performing at youth groups, in churches, and even in prisons throughout the state.

"It was uplifting to be able to reach people and encourage them through my music and through what I say to really go deeper with Him," she recollects. "I felt humbled that God would let me do that.

"We'd be going through a kind of discouraging time in the States—like Why were we here? My dad had lost his job and we were struggling. And then I sang at a prison and it was just such an incredible sense of worship—these men were so on fire for God.

"When you go into a place like that, where two-thirds of them are murderers, and then you see Christ being worshiped, it encouraged us to stay here. Seeing that was a miracle. It made us feel like we had a purpose and a mission."

That was the first of several miracles Rebecca experienced during that period of time. "We hardly had anything to our name, but we would pray as a family and miracles would take place.

"We'd get an unexpected check in the mail, or groceries would arrive at our doorstep—someone even anonymously gave us a van. Another 'angel' anonymously paid the hospital bills when my sister was born.

"It was truly miraculous," she proclaims. "We would figure out exactly how much money we needed to survive, and a check from someone would arrive in the mail for exactly that amount. It was God's grace in action.

"We never lost our faith or questioned God through those times," she recollects. "We just totally relied on God. I never blamed Him, because my parents have always said that trials can help us and shape us. We can't blame God. We don't have any right to blame God or ask why—because He's God, He's our Creator, and He knows what's best."

Perhaps one of the most incredible miracles of all was receiving a record contract at age sixteen from Forefront Records, quickly followed by the release of her debut album.

"We thanked God for that one. We were really humbled by that."

Although today Rebecca is considered one of the hottest young talents in the Christian music arena, she hasn't let success go to her head. The young star remains constantly focused on her spiritual life and says one way she does so is by a frequent reading of her favorite scripture.

"What I used to do to learn scripture is to write verses that God made stick out to me on little cards that I had in my purse or my pocket. I used to take them out and look at them or share them at the end of concerts—that sort of thing. This verse from Acts is one of those verses that I had on a card. It's always really stuck with me and really challenged me—and it still does."

Today Rebecca, who has been recognized as one of fifty up-and-coming evangelical leaders under the age of forty, won't be found cleaning houses. Instead, the Grammy and Dove nominee lives in a spacious farmhouse with her family in the Nashville countryside.

She counts her blessings and believes that not only can a reading of scripture bring blessings into other people's lives, but it can help them overcome many problems, as well.

"This scripture—any scripture—is a powerful healing tool," she offers. "It totally relates to what you may be going through. The verse from Acts asks us to focus on our mission, and it doesn't really matter how we feel. It doesn't matter about ourselves—it matters more that we're being faithful to God right where we are with everything we've got.

"These words were written by Paul, and he had so much hard stuff going on in his life. And to be able to say that 'I don't care about my own life'—I mean, wow! He really knew about suffering. . . ."

AUTHOR'S NOTE: *Christian singer-songwriter Rich Mullins was killed in a car accident on September 19, 1997, in Illinois. This interview was conducted several months before his death.*

Rich Mullins

Be not righteous over much; neither make thyself over wise: why shouldest thou destroy thyself?

Be not over much wicked, neither be thou foolish: why shouldest thou die before thy time?

It is good that thou shouldest take hold of this; yea, also from this withdraw not thine hand: for he that feareth God shall come forth of them all.

ECCLESIASTES 7:16–18

SOUNDTRACKS USED TO PLAY IN-side Rich Mullins's head that had less to do with his music and more to do with developing a deeper, heartfelt connection to the Lord.

Having struggled with everything from alcohol addiction to long years of "feeling tormented all the time," the Christian music superstar with the shoulder-length brown hair who lived in a trailer on the Navajo Indian reservation in Window Rock, New Mexico, had had plenty of time to assess his struggles, the mysteries of faith, and the true meaning of being a Christian.

And what the forty-one-year-old Indiana native, who had garnered ten Dove nominations over the past decade, had concluded in his solitary search for God was that too many overrighteous Christians try to serve the Lord with an excess of doctrine rather than by simply opening their hearts to His love and light.

"The heart of Christian faith is a radical and reasonable trust and focus on Jesus," declared the popular singer and songwriter, who, in 1997, was named Favorite Inspirational Artist by readers of *CCM Magazine*. "But for many of us our focus has shifted very subtly from love for Jesus and faithfulness to Him and obedience to Him to a set of doctrines."

Rich asserted that the verse from Ecclesiastes served to remind him to try to avoid such doctrinal extremes.

"Christianity is about a daily walk with this person Jesus," he proclaimed, "and that's why I love Ecclesiastes. The gist of the whole book is just live—live out the will of God, and live abundantly."

RICH MULLINS'S HUSKY VOICE TOOK ON A TONE of annoyance as he recalled a recent incident that illustrated what he believed was wrong with much of Christianity today.

"I was at a citywide youth rally, and one of the pastors at a meeting said 'We need to tell these kids about Jesus so that they'll stop getting pregnant, stop doing drugs, and doing all these things.'

"And I thought, 'Wow, we need to tell all these kids about Jesus because Jesus wants them to know about Him. It has nothing to do with their sexual conduct or with the management of their bodies or their minds. It has only to do with God so desperately wanting us to know that He loves us, that He incarnated himself—he became Jesus—so that we can know that.' "

That type of heartfelt contact with the Lord demonstrated much of what Rich Mullins was all about, and he made every effort to impart his feelings through his God-glorifying songs of faith and wonder.

"Jesus' message is not to be good boys and girls so that when you die you can go to heaven," he passionately proclaimed. "The message of Jesus is 'I love you. I love you so deeply it kills me.'"

Letting that light into his own heart had been a long and arduous struggle for the Christian music star—one that involved "more than ten years of darkness where I felt tormented all the time."

Rich added that his struggle was far from over, which was one reason why he lived on an Indian reservation in the first place—"to work out my own salvation with fear and trembling."

Although Rich recalled having always felt driven to know the Lord, the Cincinnati Bible School graduate also painfully remembered how he often felt spiritually empty and separated from God's love—an emotion he today believes was induced by Satan.

"I've been in and out of all kinds of things—like self-depreciation, self-interest, ego trips, alcohol, and other addictions," he declared. "I've failed many times to avoid those kinds of temptations. But that's not what the Devil was really interested in. What he was trying to do is make me feel apart from God.

"You know, I was brought up in a very rationalistic kind of family—the idea of the Devil was a little outside of our thing. It's taken me a long time to recognize that there are spiritual forces who would like to harm us. Now I know that what Satan would like most to take from us is our true knowledge of who we are—which is children of God."

It wasn't instant revelation that helped the then thirty-year-old performer pierce the darkness with God's light but, instead, a series of "small steps" that included prayer, confession, and the reading of scripture.

Rich recalled how one day he made an honest assessment of his life and found all the secret sins he was guilty of less than pleasing.

"I remember being on the road to Michigan and saying to myself 'Oh, God, why don't you just make my car crash?' "

However, instead of crashing, Rich found himself steering his car in the direction of Cincinnati, where a couple of his good friends lived. It was there that Rich unburdened his soul and began to lighten his load.

"It was really liberating," he recollected. "My struggles with addictions and the darkness I was feeling lessened. There was a renewed feeling of intimacy with God."

Subsequently, grateful to be on the road to spiritual recovery, Rich took time out from his busy schedule to share the gift of faith with Navajo children on the reservation where he lived his Thoreau-like existence. "A lot of people think I've come here to save the Indians," he offered, "but it was a desire to feel God's love out of the American mainstream."

Whether onstage or off, Rich tried to spread the message that no matter how badly people may feel about themselves— as he once did—they are never unworthy of God's love and will never be abandoned by their creator.

"Anytime that we focus on our performance, that in itself cuts us off from God—not successfully—because God's grace is greater than even our darkest sin," he declared.

"From my junior year of high school until age thirty I felt tormented all the time. I was depressed. I just think I have that sort of personality. Was I going to be kept from the Kingdom of God because I have a tendency to be morose? Or because you have a withered hand? Or because maybe you have some kind of chemical imbalance that leads to an addiction? You're not a Christian because of how you feel, you're a Christian because of what Jesus did for you."

The brown-eyed entertainer, whose laid-back stage presence often belied the spiritual intensity smoldering within him, was critical of "overrighteous" Christians who believe that only people who live so-called moral lives are eligible for salvation.

"Life and living comes from God—it comes from Jesus— not from doctrine or good morals," he declared. "You can be an utterly moral person and not be alive. Jesus came that we might have life, not good morals. It's not that I'm opposed to good morals at all, it's just that sometimes I think we put the cart before the horse."

Much of Rich's philosophy was shaped as a youngster growing up in the former Quaker settlement of Arba, Indiana. "About half the people who lived in Arba were relatives of mine." He chuckled. "My cousins lived there, my great-grandmother lived next door to us, and all my Sunday school teachers were my uncles and aunts.

"And one of my greatest influences in thinking about all this was my own father. My dad was very honest about who he was. He was very honest about his weaknesses and strengths. He never pretended to be something when he was in church that we knew he wasn't at home."

In contrast, Rich remembered himself as a kid who was almost "hyperpious." "I remember being so embarrassed by him. Then puberty kicked in, and I became aware that all of my piety—all of my devotion—was really very shallow. Somewhere deep inside me I was still very human. It was that human part of me that Jesus loved. It was not the phony part of me that I wore on the outside."

Although Rich would frankly admit that he was still not completely free from dark moments that sometimes gripped his soul, more recently he had found it easier to contend with those moments by turning to scripture.

"This scripture has come into play so many times in my life when I've fallen into those moods and the temptation of evaluating myself and saying 'How am I doing?'

"It seems that God is always saying 'I'm not worried so much about how you're doing as much as I'm glad about who you are.' The scripture also says don't get too hung up in your failures, your weaknesses, or your addictions—it doesn't make your separate from God, because He still loves you."

Rich remained convinced that scripture is a powerful tool that can help heal others as it had helped heal him. "I hope that by reading this scripture they'll feel like I do. There are so many times I've said, 'Who am I trying to fool? I may as well just quit.' Or you might be thinking 'I just can't bear this.' Then I read this scripture and it helps.

"It's helped me because what it says is this is not about your righteousness. Your righteousness is all in Jesus. So don't get so hung up about how important you are in the Kingdom of God or how important you are to the growth of the church. Just figure out where you're most alive, most vital, and go there. Enjoy the gift of life that He's given you."

The popular Christian artist did, however, add one word of caution. He warned against placing too much emphasis on the words of scripture rather than upon the one who inspired it.

"The goal is not that you should become a great Bible scholar," he asserted. "It's not about mere intellectual assent to a set of doctrines. The goal is that you should be like Jesus—and the scriptures can help you with that. I don't need to read the Bible because I'm a great saint. I read the Bible because I'll find God there. It's about a daily walk with this person Jesus."

Tony Vincent

Let no man despise thy youth; but be thou an example of the believers, in word, in conversation, in charity, in spirit, in faith, in purity.

1 TIMOTHY 4:12

ALTHOUGH STILL ONLY IN HIS TWEN-
ties, singer and songwriter Tony Vincent be-
lieves he has experienced enough "sorrow,
pain, and tears" to have something of importance to say
about life's ups and downs.

The lanky, intense, Star Song recording artist reveals that
those ups and downs have included an obsessive need always
to be in control and a near-fatal bout with anorexia—all of
which changed when he established a personal relationship
with the Lord at age fifteen.

The twenty-three-year-old Albuquerque, New Mexico, na-
tive, who released his debut album in 1995, also serves as an
outspoken advocate for his generation.

Which is why Tony asserts he selected the verse from
Timothy as one of his favorites. He believes it is wrong to
brand today's youth with such derogatory labels as "Gen-
eration X" and that this scripture addresses such negative
attitudes toward the young.

"It's my responsibility where I am as an artist to let people
know that being young doesn't have to have such a negative
connotation," he declares forcefully. "We can still be very
effective in loving people and changing lives.

"This verse is the only one for me that is a mission state-
ment. It says don't let anybody look down at you because

you're young. I think it's a verse that will change people's lives—I know that it has changed mine."

TONY VINCENT'S VOICE TAKES ON AN EMOTION-al fervency as he talks about how angry he becomes each time he hears members of his generation described as being uncaring. "I really don't agree with that at all," he attests. "I think we really have a lot of individuality to share.

"I think our generation has taken a lot of heat from the media because, it's true, we have a lot of wild stuff going on, but I think every generation always does. Our generation seems to be either more vocal or more in the eye of the masses. They try to loop us all into one demographic—myself included—and I don't think that's right.

"And this verse from Timothy—'don't let anybody look down at you because you're young'—says to me, 'You know what? Just because this is the perception of my generation doesn't mean that I have to be stereotyped as this kind of person.'"

The unmistakably talented six-foot-tall singer with the mature, articulate voice will admit that there is a certain void in the lives of many young people, one that he hopes to fill through his music with songs like "Do You Really." It's a song, the star explains, about transcending that void and looking for the eternal perspective of things.

"What I feel is a lot of emptiness in my peers," he submits. "Relationships that should have been in place have never been there with a lot of young people. That's why my generation hasn't gone bad, they're just very empty—they just don't know any different.

"And I'm trying to provide motivation for them to question where their position is in life. I'm trying to provide that eternal perspective—to give them something to think about after the show. I want them to think about what makes my songs personal to them and to become part of the work itself, just like in the good book."

Tony hopes to set a further example to his generation by remaining true to who he really is through his music. "I think they need honesty above anything else—more than just immediate gratification," he declares.

The "emptiness" that the young pop artist often talks about is something that he clearly recalls having once experienced himself. That feeling changed, Tony submits, when, at age fifteen, he was suddenly filled with the spirit of the Lord.

"While I went to Roman Catholic Church every Sunday morning with my parents and my sister, it really didn't mean anything to me," he recollects. "I was just hopefully doing the right thing and earning my way into heaven by going to church.

"I didn't understand what having freedom in Christ was all about, or even knowing God on a personal level. I didn't even know that God wanted to have a personal relationship with me. I had never heard that before."

When a friend invited the teenager to attend a Baptist church service, Tony remembers how his whole world suddenly changed.

"I came from a works-based religion and this was all very different for me," he asserts. "I thought if you walked as many ladies across the street that you could, or whatever charity events you participated in, that it would hopefully get you to heaven.

"But you wouldn't know if you were going to get there until you were standing at the gate. For the first time I found out that Christ's love for us is unconditional and that His sacrifice on the cross is all we need. I was now at a place where I felt that I didn't have to earn my way into heaven— and that was a totally different perspective than I had growing up.

"Learning that was finding real inner peace—the fact that we don't have to earn our way into heaven was a very restful thing for me. I learned that my security was really based on the grace of God, not on what I did."

Tony relates that four months later he and his entire family joined the Baptist church. "Now for the first time as a family we became intimate with God. We developed an individual relationship with our Heavenly Father. We weren't getting that with the Catholicism that was taught at the church we attended."

He also remembers purchasing a Bible for the first time after he became a Baptist and beginning an individual and structured reading of the holy book. "I had never owned a Bible before," he attests. "I didn't know that anybody but the priest could read from the Bible.

"Having my own Bible and starting to go to Sunday school really started to establish a foundation that just gave me an understanding of what God really did—why He did what he had to do, like dying on the cross. I actually found that the Bible could be fun and interesting."

Tony also recalls how impressed he was at discovering the power and inspiration that scripture offered—particularly how forgiving those words were. "I had no experience with that," he offers. "All I knew before was that God was condemning. And that is really contrary to what this book says. I discovered that our God is a real gracious God."

What further impressed him about the Baptist church was the music that he heard performed during the services. "I didn't have a spiritual foundation when it came to music," he relates. "I was raised in mainstream radio.

"I knew that music was what I wanted to do for a living—

whether it was within the church or out. But the fact that God could play a part in it was a very freeing thing to hear."

Tony can still remember how awed he was the first time he sat in church and listened to a thirty-piece orchestra backing up a twenty-five-member youth choir. "I didn't even know that was ever allowed in church. In our church services we were lucky to even have an acoustic guitar." He chuckles.

"So I started asking questions like 'Wow, this kind of stuff can happen in church? Why is that? Why don't they get offended by loud drums and stuff like that?' And seeing this kind of thing performed in a church in this magnitude, that's what changed my life. It really opened the doors of my consciousness."

Although music had always been his calling, for Tony it was a question about which direction that love for music would take him. At age two he was already displaying his remarkable talents, performing in stage productions, musicals, in concerts, and on radio and television.

But now, at age fifteen, the youngster began giving serious thought to a career that blended his love of music and ministry. "I wanted to do something that would get people to start thinking about their heart and where eternity lies for them," he asserts.

Tony recalls that as he grew into his new relationship with

God, many of the personal problems he was struggling with—particularly his compulsive need to control everything and everyone—tended to lessen.

"I was always trying to control my image before others, trying to control my relationships, my business deals, et cetera," he recollects. "I was doing that instead of resting in the person and provision of Christ."

Nowadays Tony no longer tries so hard to "make it happen." Instead, he is "being who I am in the Lord, and seeing what happens. That's still a very difficult thing for me to grasp because I was raised to be a hardworking individual— that it's the result of your work that got you to the places that you wanted to be. So I still fight a lot with giving control over to my God."

The handsome singer and songwriter also credits scripture for helping him to survive a devastating bout with anorexia. "Back in my last year of high school I dealt with this," he submits. "I was a six-foot individual and down to about 123 pounds. It was because I felt that my life was empty and out of whack and that the food portion was basically all I could control."

Tony remembers how that began to change when he started reading scripture, combined with prayer and counseling. "That's when I think my relationship with God became not head knowledge but moved into my heart. Because I know I was on this road heading to nowhere. I was basically killing my body off. Now that situation was changing."

Reflecting back upon that struggle, Tony sees that some good came of it. "While that situation was bad, today I think of it as a positive thing that brought me closer to the Lord. The Lord helped to dig me out of the hole I was in."

Returning to his soapbox about today's youth, the young entertainer, who is married and the father of one child, suggests that any young person who feels alienated from society read the verse from Timothy because it will result in a healing.

"The whole thing about finding purpose in life is important to people. And if we don't feel significant, we're just empty. This verse helps to fill people—it helps to change people's lives. It changed mine."